Napkins

Lunch Bag Notes From Dad

By Courtney Garton

Acknowledgements

To my daughter, Cara, thanks for caring enough to save the napkins.
Without them, there would be no *Napkins*.

To my daughter, Adrienne, thanks for valiantly paving the way for your sister.
I know it was hard being the first born.

To my mother, Audrey Garton, thanks mom for raising me right, and for setting the
example of a loving parent.

To my former spouse and the girls' step-mother, Margie Bryce, thanks for a lot,
not the least of which is giving me the time to spend with the girls while they were growing up.

To my former spouse and the girls' mother, Mary Petersen, thanks for our beautiful creations.

To my friend Lynne Murphy, thanks Murph for your encouragement, and for finding me a publisher.

To my editor and friend, Lucy Oppenheim of Oppenheim Editing, thanks for organizing my writing,
and rescuing me from computer hell.

To my editor, Peter Porosky, thanks for prodding me to dig deeper to remember the details.
Your comments and criticism truly inspired me.

To my publisher, Marsha Berman of Perry Publishing, thanks for having confidence in *Napkins*.

To my brother-in-law, Clay Butterworth, thanks for the moving endorsement.   ☺

Parent's Prayer

"I seek your forgiveness for all the times I:
 Talked when I should have listened;
 Got angry when I should have been patient;
 Acted when I should have waited;
 Feared when I should have been delighted;
 Scolded when I should have encouraged;
 Criticized when I should have complimented;
 Said no when I should have said yes and
 Said yes when I should have said no. "

—*Marian Wright Edelman*

To my daughters,
and my mom.

"Between the dark and the daylight,
  When the night is beginning to lower,
  Comes a pause in the day's occupations
  That is known as the children's hour."
  —*Henry Wadsworth Longfellow*

Introduction

On May Day 1970, on that tumultuous weekend, as kids were dying in Vietnam and being shot dead at a Kent State University anti-war demonstration on campus, my flower child of a daughter, Adrienne Peace, was born.

On Valentine's Day 1973, on that cold, Cupid Wednesday, as a heartless, arctic air mass knifed southward and froze lovers' romantic hopes of an early spring in Annapolis, my sweetheart of a daughter, Cara, was born.

A year later, the girls' mother and I separated. When Cara was three, the divorce was final, with legal custody of both Cara and Adrienne being granted to their mother.

The visitation arrangements were that I would get the girls for an overnight every Thursday and, every other week, from Thursday through the following Monday morning. At that time, I was a high school teacher with summers off. Because of my flexible schedule, the divorce judge granted that the girls live with me for six weeks during their summer vacations.

This liberal visitation arrangement gave me the opportunity to be more than just a "weekend daddy." For one thing, it allowed me to experience the logistical challenges of getting the kids up and off to school every Friday morning and alternate Monday mornings. Neither Adrienne nor Cara relished eating the school cafeteria meal, so included in my early a.m. routine were making and packing their lunches.

I liked the continuity of long term visits. They allowed me to get into Cara's and Adrienne's lives in a way which would not have happened if their visitations had been cosmetic. Cara was never one to tread lightly on sensitive ground. She validated my feeling that I was as much a part of her and Adrienne's reality as their mom by insisting that she had two homes, Dad's and Mom's. She also became indignant whenever Adrienne innocently referred to her mom's house as home. "A-Dree-Ann," Cara would admonish, "Dad's house is just as much home as Mom's." Adrienne would waveringly agree, and then rejoin, "Yeah, but we *live* with Mom." On and on, the argument would continue about what constituted a "home," until one of them would tire and throw up her hands with a dismissing "whatever," and that would be that.

In 1977 I re-married. My wife Margie helped enormously with raising the children; she also spent many hundreds of hours taking care of our then newly started retail hat shop business, *Hats in the Belfry*, so that I would have the time to spend with Adrienne and Cara.

Our early school-morning breakfasts were my favorite times. On Friday and Monday mornings, I usually woke up around six, went into the kitchen, set the table, poured three glasses of left-over Minutemaid orange juice, and hard-boiled four eggs. While the eggs were cooking, I scoured the refrigerator for lunch bag entrees. The previous night's vegetable lasagna could be eaten cold, and those pre-cut pasta squares fit nicely into a clear plastic sandwich baggy. A few unscraped carrot cuts and two trimmed celery sticks, accompanied by a tablespoon of blue cheese salad dressing, made nice appetizers. A tart green apple, sliced into thin wedges, for Cara, and an individual box of Rice Crispies from the Kellogg's 12 Pack Variety of Cereals for Adrienne, sufficed for dessert. By then, the eggs had boiled. With animated gestures that would have made a pancake-flipping, greasy spoon, short-order cook envious, I hastily peeled the eggs, allocated two to a plate, and while still steaming hot, fork-mashed them with a dab of butter and a sprinkle of salt and pepper. Just as I tossed the eggshells into the mini compost pail located under the sink, the English muffins popped out of the toaster. A slab of Welch's Grape Jelly onto the muffins, a hearty yell upstairs to the girls that it was time to eat, and a typical day for me with the girls had begun.

At that surreal hour of the day, clarity of thought wasn't always my main ingredient. But after breakfast, when I was putting the finishing touches on their lunches, I usually remembered to include a napkin in the bag. I don't know how I became so obsessed with making sure that they would have a napkin. Perhaps my serviette fixation harkened back twenty five years to the days when I took my bag lunch to school and inevitably, there would be a sloppy PB&J sandwich, wrapped in wax paper, neatly folded, with way too much strawberry jam oozing out from the tanbark Wonderbread crusts. I could never pick up my sandwiches without getting sticky stuff all over my hands, and if there was no napkin, I'd have to lick my fingers. It was just one of those little irritations that I endured as a child. I tucked this lack away in my memory and vowed as a parent never to foist it onto my own children.

Like many parents, I was kid-raising by the seat of my pants, with a little help from some books I'd read and courses I'd taken. I knew little about parenting, and I wasn't reticent about admitting it. There were numerous times in my relationship with Cara and Adrienne when I did not pay attention to the important and over reacted to the trivial. I was too lenient on them when they were impudent to their step-mother and too harsh if they violated curfews. All too often, if I had a problem with their behavior, I was judgmental in my discussion of the issue. "You know it was wrong for you to tell your sister you *hate* her," I'd censure the offender. "You two should love each other." If caught in a situation where my textbook learning about parenting failed, I resorted to the way my parents had raised me. Many times, I was in the dark, groping for neat, packaged solutions but as is often the case with the subjective, I couldn't find simplistic answers to complex challenges, such as what to do about sibling rivalry, or poor performance in school because of a personality conflict with the teacher. Trying to be a good father frequently frustrated me.

But I did have some tools. A college sociology professor once told me that much of what he thought comprised good parenting was simply paying attention to your children. I thought that he'd given me pretty solid advice and incorporated "pay attention" to a few other parenting rules which I had learned, like "no spanking." I also thought about what I wanted the end product of my parenting to be — what could I reasonably expect that my kids be like at the end of their eighteen to twenty-one year apprenticeship with me as one of their "guiding lights."

I thought it entirely reasonable to establish as a goal that Adrienne and Cara *survive* — that is, that they be alive and healthy at nestleaving age. I also thought that their chances of happiness in life would be greatly enhanced if they did not become pregnant and if they got college educations. Finally, I put a very high priority on the possibility that the girls and I would have a good relationship when they became adults. I thought that this accomplishment would depend on how I treated them while they were growing up.

That was it. Alive, healthy, not pregnant, educated, and baggage free of father-inflicted emotional damage. That's what I would shoot for.

One tactic I used was to allow the girls as much decision making power as possible. One slightly chilly Sunday morning in late April, for instance, when Cara was maybe three, she dawdled with her dolls instead of getting dressed for brunch at a popular, downtown deli. When I reminded her that we'd be leaving soon, she defiantly responded that she was not putting on a top and skirt, that she was going in her underwear. Rather than getting into a lose-lose shouting match with her, when time came to go, I simply picked her up, with only her underwear on, plopped her onto the cold back seat of our 1970 white Nash Rambler, threw a Mickey Mouse T-shirt, Donald Duck sweater, and Goofy pants onto the seat beside her, and drove off. She never complained that she was cold, but when we reached the deli, she had miraculously become fully dressed! (Except that I'd forgotten her shoes). The key was that I had respected Cara's demand on a non-critical matter, and although I really didn't want her to sit through brunch half naked, I was prepared to let her decide how much clothing to put on. Our potential clash of wills turned out to be a win-win experience for us both.

Similarly, if the girls wanted to wear one blue sock and one red one, fine with me. I just wasn't going to get into a power struggle with them about subjects as personal as their clothes or jewelry. The hassle wasn't worth it. More than once I heard, "Whose body is it anyway, Dad?" — their taunting yet legitimate refrain when I sometimes tried to usurp their power by imposing my time schedule onto their agenda. Like the time I tried to convince them to wait until their sixteenth birthday before getting their ears pierced. Now that they are adults, Adrienne and Cara may have a different remembrance than I about those growing up years and how much freedom I allowed them, but with the guidance of their step-mother, I earnestly attempted to let go of the authority rope and let them make their own mistakes and feel the resulting consequences. I don't mind admitting that, although the theory was sound, its execution was too often lacking.

The teenage years were the most difficult. During this part of my girls' development, it seemed as if common sense, reason, and rationality had flown out the window. Being with them was like living in a combination fun house/insane asylum. There was always something unexpected happening, and I felt that either they were crazy or I was.

Early on, I found that I could cope better with the hurly-burlyness of child rearing if I just let go and allowed myself to gravitate to my own inherent strata of derangement. For you see, from time to time, I had caused friends and family to reflect on whether my mind was cruising on all cylinders. Like when I quit my stable teaching and math department head position of eight years and, overnight, dove into the retail hat business. And certainly, in 1978, when I purchased a delivery vehicle, a purple, 1962 Cadillac hearse, to haul hat boxes from home to the shop. I bought the coffin carrier for a hundred bucks from the Annapolis Elks Club — then spent three thousand dollars outfitting it with essentials such as a new battery and an engine overhaul, and fancy accoutrements like six inch thick foam-padded, plush red carpeting to cover the casket casters in the rear, custom, calico-colored window curtains, and a high-tech, West German, sen-surround stereo system. Having bought the dying jalopy about the same time as the famous Hearst kidnapping occurred, I christened my bargain burial buggy "Patty (the) Hearse." Patty had our *Hats in the Belfry* logo painted on three of her five doors, and she could haul forty hat boxes or eleven (living) people in her coffin compartment. On Sundays, we'd pile a case of Bud and ten friends in the back, and motor up Main Street and around the Markethouse in downtown Annapolis. On the way home, for a lark, I'd drive Patty, with her load of partially plastered passengers, through the Crown Station automatic car wash. It was pretty cozy, eleven of us in there, huddled, suddenly all quiet, watching and listening as those huge whirring brushes and drenching waterfalls transformed Patty the Hearse from a dirty junker to a clean one. Because of my history of zany escapades like that, I can't say for sure whether I came to parenthood a little "touched," or if the kids made me nuts. I do know that, as a father, I found myself in a topsy turvy world of toddlers and teenyboppers, a Wonderland of tots and that I, now the Mad Hatter, was delighting in the disarray.

I liked the fact that raising kids was a disheveled ordeal rather than an orderly process. In what other arena would endless euphemisms like "pee-pee," "poo-poo," "tampon," and "boys" become enshrined as household words? Being a messy person myself, I was on familiar ground. In fact, fatherhood was a safe place for me to let out the silly child in myself, as when I let the girls "fix me up." This phrase was their description of a ritual which consisted of them dragging out pink hair curlers, some old-fashioned bobby pins, tiny, multi-colored rubber bands, blue plastic barrettes, and probably the kitchen sink too, and then affixing all this paraphernalia to my head while I stoically sat in their pretend hair salon chair. When completed, all I needed was a clear shower cap, and I could have passed for Lucy Ricardo, just before turning in for the night, sitting in front of her gold embossed vanity mirror, softening her wrinkles with Jergen's overnight facial cream. Entertaining my daughters in such wacky ways drew them closer to me, and pretty much kept them guessing, in a good-natured way, about whether their father was playing with a full deck. I loved to keep them off balance. (You have to, you know, otherwise they'll eat you alive).

Of course, all this appearing to be off-kilter on my part was only about non-crucial issues in the girls' lives. If the matter at hand didn't involve their safety, health, education, pregnancy, or future relationships, I didn't see much reason to appear completely rational. Sometimes I embarrassed them with my antics, like the time I picked Cara and two girlfriends up from play practice after school, wearing my bicycle helmet for protection "just in case the car crashes." Adrienne was particularly abashed, on the last Saturday night every October, at my refusing to set the clocks back one hour like the rest of the country did, to go off Daylight Savings Time.

Instead, I would "save" the hour Saturday night, and set my clocks back on the following Sunday night, when I would need the extra sixty minutes of sleep a lot more because of having to go to work that next Monday morning. "Good grief, Dad," she'd fret, "you can't amass *time*. Be like everybody else in the world and set the clocks back Saturday!" But, naturally, I wouldn't, and she'd turn beet red whenever I publicly boasted of my ingenious time-accumulating habit. And, of course, I'd sing to the girls, anytime, anywhere, alone or in the company of others. I made up silly ditties about them and our cats, and would croon about the BEE-U-T-FULL Chesapeake Bay, the harvest moon or whatever else occurred to me. One standard tune became known as "The Grocery Store Song." Neither girl wanted to be mentioned in its name-interchangeable first line. They both sighed with dismay every time I sang it, so I sang it often. It went like this:

The Grocery Store Song

Adrienne Pee-ece Gar-r-ton
Went to the grocery store,
Said to the man behind the counter,
Oh please, oh please won't you give me some more?
The man looked at her and said,
"Little girl, what's wrong with your head?"
Adrienne looked at him and said,
"I-I-I-I don't know."

Yes, sometimes I mortified them with my monkeyshines, but despite a few inconsequential failures, they knew I was in their corner and loved them as unconditionally as I could.

So what does all this have to do with napkins?

Well, in the mornings when I fixed the girls' lunches, I decided to write them a rhyme on the napkins that I stuck in their lunch bags. I began this practice when Adrienne was about six and continued it for both girls from the time Cara started school to when she graduated from high school. I used this medium to get across my fatherly messages of love, encouragement, frustration, celebration, advice, joy, reprimand, philosophy, and other tidings that I happened to have on my mind at that dark hour of six o'clock in the morning.

Year after year, I'd scribble these poetic missives onto the kitchen tissues and stick them into the girls' lunch bags. Finally, when Cara left home for college in 1991, my rhythmic ritual came to an end.

One day in 1995, after she had graduated from college and secured a good job, Cara presented me with a shoe box full of old, yellowed, wrinkled napkins. She had saved 150 of them. Cara gave them to me as a "going away present" — as she set out to make her own way in the world. As she headed for her car, she looked back over her shoulder at me standing in the doorway, holding the shoe box, and with a little smirk, challenged, "Hey Dad, why don't you write a book?"

So, I did. My original intent was not that the book would be about fatherhood, but would simply be about the poems I had written on Cara's napkins — Cara's only, because hers were the only ones I had. Even though I "wrote napkins" for both Adrienne and Cara throughout their school years, each napkin had a different poem for each girl. It never occurred to me that the girls would save some of their poems. But Cara did, and it is because I have *her* napkins that I am able to remember more of the events in her life.

Although I rarely dated the napkins, of those that Cara kept, the earliest one that I can determine with any surety was written sometime in 1981, when Cara was eight. She did not save every napkin, and most of the poems that she gave me had been composed during her teenage years.

I almost (but not quite) feel embarrassed calling these lines of worse verse "poems." They're really no more than just scatterbrained musings that I coerced into sometime rhyme. Obviously, some are quite awful by normal poetic standards. But they were fun to write and occasionally gave Cara's cafeteria school chums a little midday anticipation and a chuckle or two. Her lunchtable friends would ask, "Hey Cara, whatdya dad write on the napkin today?" and Cara, with some pride and a little trepidation, would read the poem out loud for the whole table to hear. Her friends especially liked it if they were referred to by name on the napkin of the day.

The real value of the napkins, of course, was that they made both Cara and Adrienne feel special. The girls could tell I was thinking about them, that I was trying to be in tune with them, that I was enjoying playing with them during their sometimes difficult journey through life and, most importantly, that I loved them very much.

So, here are the napkins. I have all 150 with me, at my house, still in the shoe box. For this book, I picked the fifty or so which I felt conveyed a fair sampling. I hope you enjoy reading them as much as I enjoyed writing them.

Early Hats in the Belfry *advertisement photo of "Patty the Hearse" with Cara's daycare comrades adorning the latest in 1978 fashion headwear. Adrienne is standing on Patty's hood, wearing a top hat, holding a cane, and scratching who-knows-what. Cara is sitting third from right on the roof.*

"Pretty much all the honest truth telling there is in the world is done by children."

—*Oliver Wendell Holmes*

Lunch Bag Notes

"Daddy, daddy, we're here and we're expensive."
—*Malcolm Bradbury*

For the girls, one of the most annoying aspects of coming to visit their father every week was that they had to bring something to wear to school the following day. On alternate weeks, when Cara and Adrienne would be staying with me through the weekend, they needed to bring not only school clothes, but also play clothes, possibly dress clothes, appropriate shoes, school books, makeup, and all sorts of stuff they might need while spending that much time away from their mother's house. In other words, they were continually packing suitcases, duffel bags, and laundry bags at their mom's house, unpacking them at my house, then, after their visit with me concluded, packing again to return to mom. One particular Sunday night, Cara was loudly complaining about having to pack up again. The next morning, I empathized with her situation.

Sent Packing

Suitcase full of clothes,
Back and forth you goes,
From one house to another,
From yo daddy to your mother,

It's pack, unpack, pack, unpack.
Forth and back—your stuff in a sack.
Forget a dress and get some flack.

After all these years (and tears)
You must now have the knack
Of how to pack.

Love, dad

"Seek the wisdom of the ages, but look at the world through the eyes of a child."

—*Ron Wild*

One Halloween, when Cara was seven or eight, I had taken her and Adrienne to tour a Jaycees' sponsored "Haunted House" located about eighteen miles south of Annapolis. There were the usual ghosts and goblins but, unknown to me, the organizers had added some pretty bloody, grotesque "dead" bodies along the pathway through the house. Looking at these horrible creatures was frightening enough. Cara was clutching me tightly as we moved quickly along the morbid route. As we passed within a couple of feet of the corpses, they suddenly jumped up from their "dead" state, screamed bloody murder, and began groping toward us in a most menacing manner.

Adrienne was older, and she had seen such things before, so she thought the whole show hilarious. Little Cara, on the other hand, although trying hard to brave it like her big sister, was shaking with fear and commencing to whimper. Needless to say, we got out of there very quickly. Later, on the way home, I explained how it was all "pretend," and before we reached Annapolis, Cara fell asleep. A few days later, I wanted to touch base with her about the experience.

Treat... or Trick?

The Haunted House was scary,
its walls dark and dreary.
It made you very leery,
Almost even teary,

And, at the end, quite weary.

Love, dad

"Even when freshly washed and relieved of all obvious confections, children tend to be sticky."

—*Fran Lebowitz*

Each year for the past twenty five, tens of thousands of pedestrians have strolled across the Bay Bridge, that magnificent, four mile Chesapeake Bay span linking the eastern and western shores of Maryland. The year when Cara was three and Adrienne six, Margie and I decided to see if we could trek the distance with the girls. We knew it would be a long haul for them, but we thought they could do it, and that they would appreciate the certificate of accomplishment issued by the authorities. They would receive the certificates upon completion of the walk.

To encourage the girls to actually walk the distance, and not whine to be carried by me or Margie, we took along eight tootsie rolls, one each to be distributed to the girls at every mile marker over the bridge and at the finish. It was quite a long hike for a three year old, and after only half a mile, Cara was tired and, predictably, asked to be toted. We urged her on, promising that delicious chocolate candy at the one mile designation. Then Adrienne began to complain as well and, on that cold, blustery May day, it was all we could do to get them both across the bridge, one agonizing mile at a time, before they threw a hissy fit. We have a great picture of both girls, huddled side by side, bundled up in heavy coats with hoods which came to a point at the top, sitting along the rail on the very apex of the bridge, at the half-way mark, sucking on two partially devoured tootsie rolls, smeared chocolate wreathing their cold, wind-whipped mouths.

We did complete the walk, the girls received their diplomas, and the walk must not have permanently pocked their personalities because about four years later, this time on a warmer morning, Cara, her playmate Tracey, some other friends from our community of Bay Ridge, and I, enjoyed the Bay Bridge Walk again.

Heyday on the Bay

Yesterday we walked the big bridge,
and the day was so much fun.
We saw lots of people from the Bay Ridge
on the walk—they were enjoying the sun.

Then Trace came over for the day—
A perfect way—
—her stay—
—after the bay—
to end the day.
Hey?

love, dad

"It goes without saying that you should never have more
children than you have car windows."

—*Erma Bombeck*

At about the age of eleven, Cara embraced gymnastics. Her small, lithe, but muscular frame made her a natural, yet a natural who worked diligently to master the taxing equipment. She was determined, and looked upon each new obstacle as a challenge. She steadily improved, despite numerous, nagging ankle and wrist injuries and an intimidating coach who screamed at the gymnasts more than Vince Lombardi yelled at his Green Bay Packers football team. Still, after a year, Cara qualified for the state meet. In the weeks leading up to the big competition, she bore down. The four inch wide balance beam was the most dangerous and frustrating event for her, exacting equilibrium, execution, and poise for a top finish. I tried to capture a little of what she was thinking about with this napkin.

Meet. Your Fate?

Next week
is the big meet.
What will be your fate
at the State?

It would seem
that the beam
is the hardest.

So soar
around the floor.
Fly far
on the bar.

Somersault
over the vault.
Then it won't be your fault
if you aren't on the beam
on the beam.

love, daddy

"A torn jacket is soon mended, but hard words bruise the
heart of a child."

—*Henry Wadsworth Longfellow*

During Cara's gymnastics tenure, weight constantly ate away at her accomplishments. Every gained pound made it more difficult for her to hoist herself on the high bar or perform the required number of chin-ups, to say nothing of the ridicule the coach heaped upon her as the quite public scales displayed her increased weight before the start of each practice.

"Hey Garton," he'd bellow as the scale needle slid upwards - half a pound higher than her previous weigh in - "you watchin' your weight?" When Cara responded "yes," the coach further chided, "What - watchin' it go UP?" Cara couldn't win. If she lost weight, the coach was still on her case. "Well, now I guess we'll have to call you 'Gar-pound' instead of 'Gar-ton', huh Cara?"

Cara, of course, was developing normally. But the coaches were, in my mind, sickly focused on their prodigies staying pygmy short and rail slight. Perhaps the sport demanded it. But, as father of an aspiring athlete, there was just too much poundage pressure put on the girls for me to stomach. So, I became a little concerned the day Cara announced that, in order to lose pounds and/or maintain her weight, her meals from then on were to consist of a fruit drink and a multi-vitamin.

Food For Thought

I Fear
Your idea
To lose weight
Ain't great.

'Cause just juice
And a pill
Will

Not make your bowels loose
enough, papoose.

love, dad

"You are the bows from which your children as living arrows are sent forth. Let your bending in the archer's hand be for gladness."

—*Kahlil Gibran*

At the end of a long stretch with the girls, whether it was the summer vacation or spring break, I'd anticipate the pending loss of connection and mourn the forfeiture of my morning routine. One year, on a Sunday night in late August, Cara and Adrienne were upstairs stuffing their suitcases, preparing to go back to their mother's house the next day. I entered each of their rooms, sat on their beds for a while and watched them, sometimes helping them to sort which socks should stay at my house, which sweatshirts to pack. I reflected on merry moments during their visit, and reviewed with them recent scenes like the one where, one drowsy, dog-day afternoon, Margie had told Cara that she'd pay her a quarter if Cara would: 1. scratch her back for half an hour, without saying a word, while Margie lay face down, falling asleep on the bed, 2. then leave the room so silently that Margie wouldn't wake up, and 3. play quietly by herself for an additional thirty minutes so that Margie could continue her cat nap. Cara laughed at her remembrance of Margie's request, and that elevated my melancholy a bit.

Lifting our spirits further, Cara retold, with great fanfare, a little exaggeration and unmitigated relish, the story of how rebellious Adrienne decided not to bathe for a month that summer because she wanted more control over her life, and concluded that it was her body and she should be able to decide *if* it got washed, *when* it got washed. The three of us then all chimed in with personal anecdotes of how that smelly escapade had affected us. Cara, titillated by how greasy Adrienne would allow her hair to get before shampooing, meticulously and religiously scrutinized her sister's head each night, at bedtime, like a mommy baboon picking ticks off her baby. I told Cara to be sure to find all the lice. Finally, after three weeks of dirt and grime, and amidst great pressure from the family to come clean, Adrienne succumbed to the strain and took a shower.

Despite such lightheartedness, I still felt pretty blue about the girls' leaving. To further take my mind off their impending departure, I might chatter with them about all the cool school adventures to come as they headed into a new fall term. Or, I might simply remain silent and watch them as they packed their suitcases. Aware that my helter-skelter stretch with kids was about to be replaced with a plethoric period of peace and quiet, I just wanted to *be* there with them, in the room, studying them at close range, engraving images of their physical movements and facial expressions on the tablet of my memory. The following morning, as Cara and Adrienne readied to return to their mom's, I tried to mask my sadness.

Goodbye Girl

Today is the end of your visit.
Fixing you breakfast
Is now in the past,
And I will really miss it.

Watching silly movies with you on T.V.
Giving you a goodnight kiss.
All that I will miss,
And more.

But one thing that won't bother me,
Is now I won't have to listen to you snore!

love, dad

"But there ain't nothing worse
than
the thirteens. Right On."

—*Maya Angelou*

The girls' birthdays usually found me waxing nostalgic, especially in the case of Cara, the younger. It was strange how differently I felt as each girl reached milestones in her life. Adrienne's turning thirteen, for example, was not nearly as emotionally disquieting for me as it was when Cara entered teenagehood, because I knew that Adrienne's passage wasn't final — it was for *her* but not for *me* — because three years hence, I'd be able to relive the "turning thirteen" experience all over again with Cara. With Cara, however, who was to be my last child, an early vasectomy sealing that fate, her becoming another year older meant a year of fatherhood that was permanently past...lost. It was a segment of the girls' lives, and therefore *my* time on earth, erased forever, and that passing engendered a personal feeling of mortality brought home — another year, another memorable moment, another stage or age that would never be revisited. The sense of loss was acutely poignant for me and often reduced my poetic efforts to a mishmash of mush. I think I must have shed a tear or two writing this napkin — a stain is still evident on the "f" in "life" in the last line of the poem. It was on Cara's 13th birthday, Valentine's Day, and for me the anniversary marked the end of my little girl's innocent years and the beginning of those dreaded teenage years.

Coming of Age

Thirteen years ago this Valentine,
This little girl of mine (you)
came to Earth
through birth.

You've been as good as gold
And, as you get old,
I just wanna say

that you are the ray
of sunshine
in my life every day.

Love, dad

"There are times when parenthood seems nothing more than feeding the hand that bites you."

—*Peter De Vries*

For about a six month stretch, Cara couldn't get enough to eat. She must have just become a "teen" and definitely in a growth spurt. No matter how much food I stuffed into her bag, the next day she would complain about her "skimpy lunch." Being an observant father, of course, I took notice of this phenomenon. Being an insensitive father, of course, I razzed Cara about it.

Teenage Waistland

Eating like a horse!
But, of course -
You're growing.

Which direction?
Up and down or side to side?
Getting taller or getting wide?

That we won't be knowing
until further inspection!

love, dad

"Having children makes you no more a parent than having a
piano makes you a pianist."

—*Michael Levine*

Due to her ever-increasing weight (not excessive by any sport's standards except gymnastics) and a budding interest in the opposite sex, Cara soon left the gym for the wide open, rough-and-tumble sport of lacrosse. Her bulldog persistence paid off again, landing her the prestigious "face off" position. She was very competitive and wanted to personally score. She also wanted the team to win. Early in her lacrosse career, she showed enough promise for her doting parents to surmise that maybe some bucks could be gained through her talent. College tuition dollar-signs were flashing through my mind during one game in which she excelled, and those mercenary thoughts dribbled out of my brain and onto the next day's lunch napkin.

A Good Sport

4 lacrosse goals in one game!!!
You were fire engine hot.

Now, if each time you do the same,
and you don't come up lame,
a good scholarship you will have got!

love, dad

"Behold the turtle. He only makes progress when he sticks his
  neck out."

—*James B. Conant*

I was a public school teacher for eight years, teaching math at Southern Senior High School in Anne Arundel County, Maryland. My wife Margie taught Distributive Education at Chesapeake High School, also in the county. We had been married for about a year when we went to visit Margie's family in Florida over Christmas vacation. We travelled to Key West to celebrate New Year's 1978. While there, we noticed how vibrant the place was - everyone strolling about in the warm sunshine, buying souvenirs, smiling broadly and often. We talked about what a nice lifestyle Key West offered and compared it to what we each would be facing when we returned home to Maryland's January sleet and snow. We'd have exams to give and grade, unruly pupils to deal with, and awful weather to survive. We wondered if perhaps, when we returned home, we couldn't duplicate some aspect of the Key West atmosphere that had captivated us on our vacation.

A few days after returning and settling into our academic routine, Margie announced that she'd located a small retail shop for lease on the second floor of a mini-mall in downtown Annapolis. I inspected the space, spoke with the landlord, and Margie and I decided to take the location. We impulsively signed a two year lease for $400 a month, thereby making the commitment to go into the retail business.

The only problem was, we had no idea what we were going to sell.

It was then mid-January 1978. We were scheduled to open for business February twenty fifth. Panic began to set in. We journeyed to my home town of Richmond, Virginia, walked up and down trendy Cary Street, in the fashionable West End of town, window shopping for ideas for our own shop. Margie would see a sweater in a storefront display, and ask, "How about selling sweaters?" I'd shake my head and respond, "No, not sweaters." She then spied a shirt and inquired, "What about shirts?" Again, I responded negatively. Finally, she found a man's cap in one window and said, "How about hats?"

Bingo! All of a sudden this vision appeared to me. It was just like the proverbial light bulb going off in my head. I could see the hat shop almost exactly as it looks today, with every imaginable kind of hat, for both men and women, all displayed on open shelves, with happy customers trying them on and having a fun time. I jumped up and down, shouting, "Hats! That's it! Hats!" Margie was a little taken aback by my unbridled enthusiasm, but we immediately went to a phone booth, looked up "Hats" in the yellow pages, and called a manufacturer's number. He told us to get on a train for New York and attend a fashion show being held in two days. There we'd see lots of hats to buy with which to stock our shop.

Two days later we were in New York buying hats. We knew nothing about the hat industry and virtually nothing about retailing. At the fashion show, we'd walk up to a supplier, and Margie would say, "We're going into the hat business. You've got forty-five minutes to teach us everything you know about hats." And the suppliers responded! They took us under their wings, taught us the ins and outs of hat retailing and shipped us hats (C.O.D. of course, because we had no business credit).

We needed about $17,000 to get the shop started. No bank would lend us a dime when they found out we wanted to be hat retailers. Hats were still out of fashion in 1978; nobody wore them. Banks were not going to take a chance on this wild gambit, especially considering the high percentage of small businesses that fail in their first year. But Margie and I were convinced that we could create a demand for hats if given the chance. Finally, by telling lending institutions that we wanted to take a trip around the world, and that we wanted to refurnish our entire house (both lies), we secured the necessary loans.

Our friends and family thought we had lost our marbles. They gasped, "Hats? You gotta be kidding." They gulped, "You're giving up your teaching jobs!?" And they grilled, "What in the world makes you two loony birds think the public will buy hats?" Well, I had done a little (granted, very informal) study on hat wearing. I had noticed that in the Pepsi television commercials which I'd seen recently, models were wearing a few hats. I concluded that if Pepsi thought hats could help sell their cola, then maybe they were onto a fashion idea that we could tap into. So much for market research.

The shop needed a name. Margie recalled that when she was a small child, her mother would frequently chide her whenever she did something a little wacky with the admonishment, "What do you have, Margie, bats in the belfry?" Since our loved ones thought we were crazy because of our getting into the hat business, Margie surmised that *Hats in the Belfry* would be an appropriate moniker for our daft shop. My daughter Adrienne wanted us to call the new store, *The Incredible Hat Shop*. So, one night, over a few beers with friends in our kitchen, Margie and I put those names, and a few more, up for a vote. *Hats in the Belfry* won by a four to one margin. But people liked *The Incredible Hat Shop,* too.

In a few months, March 3, 1998, *Hats in the Belfry, The Incredible Hat Shop*, will be twenty years old. Back on March 3, 1986, I "celebrated" a HATS anniversary with Cara via this napkin.

Taking Care of Business

Eight years ago today,
We first opened our shop.
The weather wasn't exactly like May -
In fact, it snowed a lot!

In hats we sold only four,
But you know what's happened since then.
It hasn't been exactly a bore,
But where will it all end...
And when???

love, dad

"We had a lot in common. I loved him and he loved him."
—*Shelley Winters*

Eventually, of course, Cara discovered boys, or they discovered her. Life was captivating enough before the would-be Romeos came knocking; after the mutual find, things really got touchy.

As the father, I couldn't get too excited about any of these guys whom Cara brought home. Sensitivity was not my strong suit when it came to sympathizing with love lost. "There are lots more fish in the ocean" and "Tis better to have loved and lost than never to have loved at all" and "If you can't be with the one you love, love the one you're with" all became my choice cliches whenever Cara's romances ended up on the rocks of teenage infatuation. And every now and then, I threw in a slightly embarrassing napkin, just so she wouldn't take her adolescent attachments too seriously. This poem concerned one of Cara's first beaus, Kevin, who was holding his affection-for-Cara-only cards a little too close to his vest for Cara's comfort. She was obsessed with whether he liked her or her best friend, Tracey. I was obsessed with what I could rhyme with "Kevin."

Loves Me...

Fee, Fi, Fo, Fum
I smell a boy named Ke-Vun.

Does he luv ya?
Or does he not?

Or does he luv
some other wo-man?

love, dad

"If love is the answer, could you please rephrase the question?"
—*Lily Tomlin*

Boys, boys, boys. Always boys. Which is how it should have been. But I was hoping that my girls would develop into strong, independent women, and not lose their identity in the arms, or to the charms, of a seductive stripling, as so many young girls do. I bought the book, *How To Father A Successful Daughter,* in hopes that I could learn how to be a more effective guide through this mine field of callow courting, and help my daughters become happy, confident women. Alas, the book admonished me to let go, observe more, and try to control less. So... I observed.

One year, there was this male admirer who was a few years Cara's junior. Cara was short, but Lawrence The Suitor was a runt. He smiled too many teeth, and his ears hadn't yet learned to lie reasonably close to the side of his head. But Lawrence possessed unquenchable self-confidence, and he strutted it. He would cockily saunter up to Cara in the school hall during change of classes, and, in his inimical wisecracker style, banter, "How about a date, *Baby?*" Cara grudgingly admired his irritating bravado, but she knew that a love-life with Lawrence was not in her crystal ball, so she'd tell the brazen shrimp to get lost. However, being a persistent little cuss, Lawrence simply would not take no for an answer when Cara coldwatered his declarations. Even though she had a more serious relationship underway with Jeff, Cara continued to be intrigued with her juvenile wooer's ardor, and I picked up on it.

E Nee, Me Nee, Mynee, Mo

Do you love Lawrence,
Or do you love Jeff?

If you had any sense,
You'd just love yo seff
(and Daddy)

love, dad

"wot in hell
   have I done to deserve
   all these kittens?"

—*Don Marquis*

At various times during the girls' development, our household consisted of a dog, Cleveland Dentyne, and after Cleveland died, combinations of cats. First there was "Black Night, Stars and the Moon, Uh-Huh", named by Adrienne at age six. Black Night was a female black and white kitten born on the Fourth of July, 1976. Margie saved her from the pound, and I guess Black Night never forgave us for that, because she was an ornery cat. She was a sneaky biter; you'd be petting her and she'd be purring as if she were in cat paradise, when, with no warning, and for no reason, she'd whirl around and sink her teeth into your hand, hard. But, in all fairness, part of Black Night's rotten nature was my fault. I am now ashamed to admit it but when she was a tiny kitten, I had taken her to our annual family "Beach Week" and dipped (my family says "threw") her in the surf. She was terrified of the breaking waves, and everyone thought that her personality was forever warped by that cruel and traumatic experience. In any event, she didn't seem to love anyone unless that person had food, and she wasn't overly pleasant to live with. What's more, she lived a very long life, about eighteen years.

When Cleveland the dog died in 1987, leaving the cantankerous cat as our only pet, the girls felt that Black Night was lonesome and might become nicer if she had a playmate. So we put the word out that we were looking for a feline addition to the family.

A friend found a tomcat at a construction sight, and strongly suggested we adopt him. Margie and I were unsure; this housing development kitten had a flea infested nose, scabs on his head, and who knew what diseases. But because he had such a sweet nature, we decided to give him a try. Our friend said she would take him if we wanted to return him after a few weeks.

We decided to name our male mouser "Trial Basis" because he was on a tryout for permanent acceptance into our home (little did we know that he was really the one trying *us* out). It wasn't long before we realized that Trial Basis was on a test run no more: we wanted him, and he seemed to want us. Now we needed another name for him. Because he had been found on a dusty building site, Cara concluded he was only one level above a junkyard dog and therefore thought "Scumbag" was appropriate. Because nobody else could come up with a better name, Scumbag stuck. After a year of verbal abuse from my sister and everyone else in the world about our crass name selection for this "dear, dear kitty", we decided to allow my eight year old nephew, Bryce, to come up with a new name for Scumbag. Because Scumbag's dirt colored fur somewhat resembled that of an aquatic rodent that he had recently seen in his science textbook, Bryce picked "Muskrat" and that name endured.

Muskrat demanded almost as much attention as the girls did. He constantly wanted to sit in my lap and shed. Or jump in the bed, climb on my chest and knead my neck at five o'clock in the morning. Or, just as the family sat down to eat, whine to be let out onto the screened porch, and then back in again. It used to make me so mad, all these "cute" cat habits.

If Curiosity Could...

Muskrat is a curious cat.
He does things which make me furious that
he did them.

Like hollaring to go outside
Just as we sit down to eat fried
apples.

Like putting his cold paws
On my warm jaws
In the middle of the night.

Like emitting a soft purr
As he sheds his white fur
On my black pants.

No wonder I raves and rants.

love, dad

"If a dog jumps in your lap, it is because he is fond of you; but if a cat does the same thing, it is because your lap is warmer."

—*Alfred North Whitehead*

Despite our wishes for a warm affiliation between the two cats, Black Night was jealous of our new tom, and stayed away from him. So we decided to adopt yet another, as a playmate for Muskrat, and named him "Larry," after one of the Three Stooges.

Cat's Cradle

We have a new kitty,
His name is Larry.
He's teensy weensy, itty bitty,
But don't be wary.

He's black and white,
Looks just like Stars and The Moon,
With sharp nails and a strong bite,
But he'll be a clawless "it" very soon.

love, dad

"Confound the cats! All cats - alway.
Cats of all colors, black, white, grey;
By night a nuisance and by day,
Confound the cats!"

—*Orlando Dobbin*

In the morning when I was making breakfast, preparing lunches and writing napkins, our cats would inevitably be slinking around, rubbing their hair-shedding backs against my legs, anticipating breakfast for themselves, and caterwauling about the need for their litter boxes to be cleaned. I felt that instead of being his castle, this man's home was a cattery. It isn't surprising then, that catcapades were so frequently napkin topics.

Catty Corner

The cats are driving me NUTS:
Blacknight, Muskrat and Larry.
They're always looking for tuna
And peeing in the petunia
plant.

I feel like committing harry-carry,
But I can't.

love, dad

Within a month, Larry died of heart failure. So, again we were faced with securing a playmate for Muskrat. We saw an ad in the newspaper for a free kitten. We went to the home of the advertiser, and found a poor family whose pet mama cat had produced a litter of fourteen babies. The one we wanted was the runt, already named, "Hope." Unfortunately, since the needy family was not financially able to care for fifteen animals, Hope and several other kittens in the litter were probably headed for euthanasia. We couldn't take more than one kitten home, but we did salvage Hope.

At that time, Jesse Jackson was running for the office of "President of the United States." I'd heard many of his speeches, saw him in person once, and was very familiar with his famous exhortations to the dispossessed. I decided to re-name our new kitten "Jesse" after the Reverend. After all, Jackson was always encouraging his followers to "Keep hope alive! Keep hope alive!" And, by golly, we *had* kept Hope alive!

Adrienne and Cara groaned and rolled their eyes toward the heavens when I told them why I wanted the name "Jesse" for our newest feline, but they cared more about getting another kitten than they did about my stupid puns, so they went along with me. Now we were back to having three pet wildcats: Black Night, Muskrat, and Jesse.

Cat Scratch Fever

The cats are on a rampage
They oughta be put in a cage.
They're tearin' up the couch
Causing the cushions to scream "Ouch!"

It's all because their food bowl
Wasn't filled the moment I awoke.
But, in the morning, my first goal
Is not a full dish of Meow-Mix,
Nix nix,
It's YOUR breakfast and lunch to fix.

love, dad

"The man with a new idea is a Crank until the idea succeeds."
—*Mark Twain*

In the early eighties, *Hats in the Belfry*, the retail hat business that Margie and I had started in 1978, was booming. A year after opening that first shop in downtown Annapolis, we were approached by leasing agents from the Rouse Company who were searching for unique, trendy, crowd-pleasing concepts for their then revolutionary festival marketplace at Baltimore's Inner Harbor, "Harborplace." Rouse offered us a deal we couldn't refuse, and on July 2, 1980, with 100,000 customers clamoring to get in, *Hats in the Belfry*'s Harborplace location was born.

Now with two shops, the pace of everyday life escalated to a frenzy. During the first opening week at Harborplace, we virtually sold out of hats. I called suppliers and pleaded with them to ship merchandise overnight. The shelves were depleted. At times, there were so many customers wanting to get into the shop, and the shop was so jam packed, that I had to post myself outside the door and allow in a customer only when another customer exited, just like a late-night bouncer would do at a popular nightclub featuring a great dance band. A line of hungry hat customers waiting to enter *Hats in the Belfry* would form at the store entrance, and that queue of patient patrons snaked all the way down the two hundred foot hallway, past *The Limited*, the teddy bear shop, a Greek restaurant, and beyond, until the line's end was completely out of sight!

The opening of Harborplace created such an international sensation, the crowds were so massive in numbers, that Margie's and my work load burgeoned to fourteen hours a day, seven days a week. We were hiring managers, training staff, buying hats, working on the floor of the shops selling hats, and paying bills. Things were so busy that I missed my one and only summer of having the girls stay with me. Adrienne and Cara stayed with their grandmother in North Carolina during that chaotic summer of 1980.

With barely enough staff to handle our first expansion, Margie and I were handed, one year later, an opportunity to open a third *Hats in the Belfry* in the prestigious Georgetown section of Washington, D.C.

Developers were constructing a chic mall, called Georgetown Park, on a prime spot on busy "M" Street. They wanted *Hats in the Belfry* as part of their tenant mix. We informed them that we didn't consider our shop Gucci-chic, and that we did not intend to change our concept to fit their very upscale architectural criteria. At first, they agreed. "We don't want you to change your look," they promised.

One August day in 1981, after we had signed the lease, we were in a meeting with the developers discussing the interior layout of our shop. Margie and I insisted on simple, formica fixtures because we couldn't afford brass and mahogany ones, and because luxury wasn't our image. We firmly believed that fixtures should take a back seat to the hats themselves. Our customers came into our shop because of the unique selection of our merchandise, not because of the quality of carpentry in our cabinets. But the designers of Georgetown Park had more elaborate, exquisite ideas for us, despite their earlier assurances to the contrary. Margie and I left that meeting knowing that we were in trouble. We had spent a considerable amount of money already in a security deposit, we had placed orders with our suppliers for thousands of hats, we had paid an architect to draw up preliminary plans, and we had hired and trained additional staff. We had shifted into major store-opening mode and now, suddenly, realized we didn't want to be part of Georgetown Park because it wasn't us.

Demoralized, we came out of the meeting, which had been held in a building on Wisconsin Avenue, walked across the street, and there before our eyes, was a "For Rent" sign in a shop window. This retail space was can't-miss, drop-dead, made-for-us desirable. It was the perfect size, had spacious, highly visible display windows, and was on heavily trafficked Wisconsin Avenue, half a block from "M" Street. We couldn't pass it up. We found the landlord, begged him to rent us the space, signed a five year lease, negotiated a release of obligations from the

Georgetown Park people, and opened our Wisconsin Avenue, Georgetown *Hats in the Belfry* in September, 1981.

Running such a runaway business as we had could have taken its toll on my time spent with the kids. Margie saw to it that the damage done was minimal. Many times she selflessly covered for me in the business so that I could have my weekends and summers with the girls. During those years when it was so important for the kids to have a father around, I was... thanks to their step-mother. Even though Margie and I are no longer married, I will always owe her for giving me the opportunity to be the kind of father I wanted to be, and for being the best step-mother two girls could ever have.

Still, business duties sometimes collided with parenting. There were occasions when I was so stressed out that I just couldn't get it together enough in the mornings to fix a balanced, nutritious lunch. Other times, in the hurried pace of tending to *Hats in the Belfry*, it would slip my mind that the girls were coming over that night, and I'd forget to shop for the lunch foods I knew they liked. In those cases, I'd throw into their bags whatever happened to be leftover in the cupboard or refrigerator, and sometimes those resulting lunches were barely above the subsistence level. Then, I'd feel guilty that I hadn't thought enough about the kids to plan for their visit or their lunch, and my dereliction-of-provisioner-duty angst would imprint itself on the day's napkin:

Nutrition Condition Red

Doin' my daily business rituals
I forgot to buy your victuals.

So today, there's no food nutricious.
Plus, what's here ain't at all delicious.

But, for me, will you please
Just eat the week old cheese
So the bones in your knees
will bees
strong?

love, dad

"I have found the best way to give advice to your children is
to find out what they want, and then advise them to do it."
—*Harry S Truman*

Cara had just reached the stage when her developing breasts made her feel self-conscious about giving me a frontal hug. It was passable to wrap my arms around her and squeeze her shoulders while she stood sideways to me, but she no longer allowed contact of her chest against mine. I knew that her modest stand toward me would pass someday so, although a little hurt that she would show such reserve toward me, her father, and not to those mischief prone boys hovering around her like a swarm of nectar sucking bumblebees, I bit my tongue and honored her qualms.

That spring, Cara and I went shopping for new clothes. Her newfound reserve in hugging her dad was conspicuously absent in her selection of outfits. I was appalled at how skimpy the cotton skirts were that she eyed, and how much skin the tank tops revealed. I was concerned that the provocative outerwear she had picked out might send the wrong message to the residing, wanton wolfpack. (Not pregnant *was* one of my absolute goals for the girls). However, trying hard to respect the delicacy of the subject, I took to lunch bag correspondence, rather than direct oral communication, to get my concerns heard.

I never knew, when I wrote a napkin like the following, whether Cara thought it funny, prying, dumb, or unnecessary, but I figured little to no feedback was a signal for me to keep on doing, so I kept on writing.

How To: Act One

You got some shorts,
You got a shirt.
"Oh yes," you retorts,
"The better I can flirt."

So, OK, cut your glances,
Play on the fancies
Of the guys.

But a word to the wise:
Overdoing it will
Bring your romances'
demise.

Love, dad

"The best inheritance a parent can give his children is a few minutes of his time each day."

—*Orlando A. Battista*

Each spring throughout high school, Cara played lacrosse. As every lacrosse parent knows, the games are always played in near-freezing temperatures with northwest winds of 20-25 knots accompanied by a bone-chilling blend of slow rain, sleet and snow flurries. Even if an hour before game time the sun shone, dressing for the game as if the weather forecast called for a blizzard was the best way to avoid frostbite (lacrosse-bite) and earache.

Cheerleading for Cara came naturally to me. She was a passionate player, and I looked forward to watching her tackle this demanding sport. So every March, I'd try to buck up her spirits with a napkin on the season ahead.

Tis the Season

Another spring of lacrosse
Has finally commenced.
Soon will be the opening toss,
Everyone'll be somewhat tensed.

But you'll snare the ball,
And drive your opponent up the wall,
As you zig and zag
Towards the net.

She'll be left holding the bag,
And you'll score - no sweat!

love, dad

"Children are one-third of our population and all of our
future."
—*Select Panel For The Promotion Of Child Health, 1981*

Cara was an excellent high school lacrosse player. She embodied a stick-with-it, stick-it-to-em tenacity that compensated for her body size shortfall. She was meticulous about hard, but fair, play and expected the same from opponents. Often, when she absorbed cheap shots, Cara's sensitivity surfaced, tears of indignation flowed, and she became discouraged. Other teams learned they could frustrate Cara by double-teaming her, and by occasionally playing (straying) just outside the rules of good sportsmanship. After one rough game in which Cara had been tripped up, knocked down, and hit hard on the head with the lacrosse stick, I knew she was seething, and I felt compelled to comment.

Games People Play

When it's the end of winter's frost
And you're back playing lacrosse
And the girls on the other team
Are mean,
And act like brutes,
No need to "put up your dukes."
Or call them "Fascist pukes!"

Try to restrain your rebukes,
Because (and this ain't news)
Lacrosse is a Game,
And life will be the same
Win or lose.

love, dad

"Children today are tyrants. They contradict their parents,
  gobble their food, and tyrannize their teachers."

—*Socrates*

On their fifteenth birthday, children should probably leave home and go live on a farm some-where for a year. Fifteen was the worst of the teenage years (at least for this parent). Cara was moody at mealtimes because she didn't want to be at "this boring banquet," and therefore, she threatened, any minute she "might barf" on the tablecloth. She sulked whenever she was sans boyfriend, and yet still sulked a great deal of the time when she was going with someone. Of course, *going* with someone meant she'd go-go-go all day and then want to stay out half the night too. When she wasn't being sullen, Cara sporadically vented spleen about not having unfettered license to come and go as she pleased. Rules were, by definition, unreasonably restrictive.

Her hopping hormones must have jumbled her usually balanced judgment, because she became quite testy and touchy concerning the topic of trust. Cara's ceaseless, rhetorical chorus, about almost anything, settled into, "You do TRUST me, don't you, Dad?" — and my perpetual refrain, about almost everything, was, "TRUST you to do what, Cara? Awaken me if you notice the house is on fire?" Then, just as I began to think that I should get more active in Cara's life in order to fos-ter smoother relations between us, she withdrew from me!! Clammed up. Tortured me with the ter-rible Silent Treatment. Switched from, "Let's go on a hike, Dad" to "Go take a hike, Dad."

I don't mind admitting that the only way I got through this turbulent time, with any degree of sanity intact, was to remember and regularly repeat to myself Beatle George Harrison's mantra, "This too shall pass. This too shall pass."

In Between at Fifteen

We don't get to talk,
Me and You,
The way we used to do.

You've got things on your mind,
And not much time,
To find
For jus' sittin a spell.

Oh well,
That's part of being fifteen,
And I know you don't mean
it.

love, dad

"We argued the thing at breakfast,
 We argued the thing at tea,
 And the more we argued the question,
 The more we didn't agree."

—*Will Carleton*

Sometimes dealing with a teenager is about as satisfying as hammering your head against a hemlock. You try everything, hoping something works. Even if one approach does work once, you can't assume that it will ever work again. You try being humorous, being stern, raising your voice, lowering your voice, appearing super concerned, appearing nonchalant. Occasionally, keeping the atmosphere cordial just doesn't pan out, and you feel like wailing lamentations to the great child-rearing god in the sky.

Upon turning fifteen, Cara suddenly began to get invitations from boys to take rides with them in their cars. The thought of a sixteen year old guy driving around with my daughter sitting beside him, perhaps driving him to distraction, presented too dangerous an image for me to emotionally incorporate. This new problem thrust itself into the family scene with lightning quickness and thundering intensity. Riding in the car with boys became of paramount importance to Cara *overnight*. I just wasn't prepared for my offspring's onslaught when I rejected her entreaty. Cara's "Car Rules," agreed upon by her mother, me, and step-mother Margie, were that she must not ride in a car with boys until she reached sixteen. For my part, I was trying to buy one more year of relatively worry-free fathering. For this stance, Cara accused me of being "hopelessly old fashioned," and "totally unreasonable." After all, she intoned, "all the other kids are doing it," and when that tired trick didn't work, she brought out her heavy guns and, thoroughly exasperated, firing point blank at my ego, screamed, "I NEVER want to be the kind of parent YOU are!"

I stuck to my own guns on this issue. The girls' safety was one of my utmost concerns, and in my mind, Cara's being in the car with an unchaperoned, hormone-driven, auto-neophyte of the teenage male variety was definitely a safety issue. One particular night, she and I heatedly rehashed the same old car argument. The next morning, having had words with her the previous evening was still on my mind.

Wishful Thinking

The teenage years are rough,
On both parents and teen.
Neither of us gets enough
of what we want—
There's no in-between.

There must be a better way
To live together each day,
With each getting our say.

love, dad

"Before . . . I had three theories about raising children. Now I have three children and no theories."

—*John Wilmot*

Sister sibling rivalry was rampant in our house. Being three years apart in age, Cara and Adrienne clearly disliked many aspects of the other's personality, and openly competed without concealing their obvious contempt for each other. As a father, it was tough at times to remain encouraged: I wanted the girls to be affectionate towards, to cooperate with, and to champion each other. I wanted Daughters Nirvana! It would depress me to get an earful of Cara's mean words spat at Adrienne, or witness Adrienne's cruel deeds earmarked for Cara.

One significant blunder which I made as a parent was that I teasingly referred to Adrienne as a frog. There was no sinister reason behind this unattractive designation. I liked frogs... thought they were cute. But Adrienne didn't. I didn't realize how touchy she was to that term, how much she hated it, until one day there occurred a nasty exchange between the girls. Cara was lying on the landing at the top of the stairs. Adrienne was down in the kitchen. Cara was berating Adrienne for borrowing her jean jacket without permission. At the end of the argument, Cara yelled, with more than a dash of vituperation in her voice, "YOU CAN'T FIT INTO MY CLOTHES ANYWAY, YOU SLIMY FROG!" Margie and I were listening to the squabble and witnessed Adrienne calmly climb the stairs to where Cara lay spread-eagle on the floor and, with a satisfied smile, stomp on Cara's stomach. With a

"Hee,hee, I got the last word," Adrienne smugly looked down at her prone, squalling sister, and sauntered into her room and closed the door.

These kinds of episodes happened infrequently, but when they did, I'd take to the napkins and preach peace, love and harmony. Preparing both girls' lunches simultaneously, I'd caution Cara on one napkin and admonish Adrienne on another. Who knows if these parental contortions to foster sibling respect relaxed the rancor or instead, fanned the flame? I do know that today, as adults, the two sisters are closer than at any point in their lives and they seem to have a real regard for each other's well being. (And nobody calls Adrienne a frog anymore).

Twisted Sisters

Try harder with your Sis,
Be extra nice - give her a kiss.

Tell her that you miss her.
She IS the only sister
That you've got.

Write her a letter,
It just might make things better.

Anyway, tis better to try
Than not.

Love, dad

"The greatest poem ever known
 Is the one all poets have outgrown:
 The poetry, inate, untold,
 Of being only four years old."

       —*Christopher Morely*

Down in the kitchen cooking in those early hours of the day — cocking an ear to determine whether the girls had turned deaf ears to their alarm clocks, eventually recognizing rustle and racket upstairs as they hustled to shower and dress — sometimes I'd feel a sense of loneliness creep up on me, and I'd grow nostalgic for the innocent years. I'd think about when the girls were little and cuddly and seemingly needed me more. It was during these reminiscent moments that I'd scribble a wishful, wistful message.

The Early Years

When you were just a little tot,
With golden, curly hair all disheveled,
You'd waddle around a lot,
Yelling, "Daddy! Look what I got!"

Your eyes would twinkle with glee
And I'd wonder, "What the devil
Is she now doing to me?"

You'd hold out your grimey, sweaty fist,
And, in it, would be a leaf or a bug.
I'd pick you up, give you a big kiss,
And you'd give me a bear hug.

So as you get on the school bus,
Remember that those days were precious,
And so are you.

love, dad

"You know children are growing up when they start asking questions that have answers."

—*John Plomp*

One particular week, Cara was grousing about some viral protuberance on her foot, namely a wart. She wondered how she'd acquired it and complained that it was marring her appearance and hampering her social mobility. My curative counsel was that she cease cavorting with frogs, but she wasn't amused. "DAAAAAAD," she whined, "it's NOT funny." Several hundred dollars in dermatologist's bills later, I tended to agree with her.

Dear Dortah

A foot with a wart-ah
Is somewhat sorta
A pain in the butt
As well as the futt.

I get the bill
And you get the thrill
Of having it removed.
That wart doesn't behoove
Either one of us

love,
daddy wart bucks

"There's a time when you have to explain to your children why they're born, and it's a marvelous thing if you know the reason by then."

—*Hazel Scott*

Cara's nickname, almost from the day she was born, had been "Cara Beara." At first, the "beara" part signified what a cute, cuddly, cub-like child she was, very warm and affectionate, so much so that it was extremely hard for me to resist constantly picking her up and giving her a gentle (bear)hug. Later, as an adolescent, the bear appellation came to represent her special degree of tenaciousness - her resolve to dig deep when the honey jar seemed empty, as when she was faced with a teacher who had no sympathy for her busy social schedule and piled on the homework, and her fighting spirit, especially when cornered, as when she absorbed a series of slamming body checks on the lacrosse field.

But — the teenage bear still sometimes got the blues. Her feeling funky could have resulted from a friend's slanting glance, a missed goal from three feet out, or a selected boy's unreturned overture. Sometimes her melancholy manner manifested itself because her car's tail pipe happened to fall off at a busy intersection while driving a carload of classmates to school, or because she felt she didn't spend enough social time with her friends, or because she conceived that her wardrobe was incurably crammed with crummy clothes or because she was simply broke.

As a father the question was, how should I treat my daughters's despondent days? Try to cheer her up, buck her up, suck up to her, what? Probably just listening worked best most of the time. No solutions, no fixes, just a sympathetic shoulder. Of course, hindsight into coping with all these pubescent psychological predicaments is a lot simpler than at the time they were festering. This napkin originated because Cara had an algebra mid-term exam and two research papers which were all due on the same day. I wanted to remind her of the significance of her nickname.

Just Do It

When times are tough,
And life is rough,
And you've had enough,

Don't get in a huff,
Don't sit on your duff,
Don't let your sails luff,

Bear Down, Bear!!!

love and kisses,
dad dee

"Not a shred of evidence exists in favor of the idea that life is serious."

—*Brendan Gill*

For me, one of the more memorable experiences of Cara's and Adrienne's teenage years was teaching them how to drive a car. This was truly risky business, both for the father-daughter relationship and for goal number one of my child rearing philosophy: survival. The place where I decided to teach the basics of motoring was the local junior high school parking lot. It was spacious, and contained no easy obstacles to crash into. It also had a curb suitable for parallel parking. The girls could make learning mistakes without dire consequences.

From the beginning, I felt that if the girls could learn to drive *backward*, then driving forward would be a snap for them. So, for a week, every day we went to the parking lot, where I instructed them to do all their practice driving in reverse. Around and around we would go, backward, the girls' necks getting cricks in them from constantly peering over their shoulders. And not only had they to learn to drive in reverse, but they also had to drive a car with a straight stick. I figured to make it as hard on them as I could so that once they actually took to the road, they would find mastering *those* skills relatively simple.

I don't know that Adrienne and Cara found learning to drive in reverse all that unusual. By this time, they knew that their father was kind of strange anyway, and after all, they were teenagers who had arrived at the age of automobile autonomy. So it probably wouldn't have mattered to them if Jack the Ripper was the one teaching them to drive. They just figured that they would endure whatever indignities were thrust upon them in exchange for the grand prize of emancipation by car.

The only negative of teaching the girls to drive in reverse came when Cara went to take her driving test. She did beautifully parallel parking, navigated her three point turn flawlessly, and was cruising along during the "back it up" stage of the test when suddenly her instructor shouted, "That's it! Pull the car over. You failed the test."

Cara was flabbergasted. She thought she'd done everything perfectly. Well, the instructor informed her, she had done everything perfectly except one thing: she was going 35 miles per hour in reverse — in essence, speeding backwards, and that was an automatic, immediate disqualifer. The driver's education teacher said in his twenty year career, he'd never had a case of someone failing the driver's license test for using excess speed in reverse. Cara was livid, and blamed guess-who for her failure? The next week, she re-applied, passed the test, and received her permit, but I still thought she could use some auto advisement.

Checklist for Starting Car

1. Be sure you know where you are.

2. Put in neutral or press in clutch
   (that doesn't require very much).

3. If it's dark, turn on lights
   (Concentrate on that with all your mights).

4. And so that you won't stall,
   Release hand brake 'fore headin' to the mall.

5. Finally — and I don't mean to be terse —
   Never go over 10 miles per hour in reverse!!

love, dad

"Your children will see what you're all about by what you live
rather than what you say."

—*Wayne Dyer*

Cara was a penny-pinching miser who, by the time she was sixteen, had saved fifteen hundred dollars for a car, *and she would not be denied*. Suddenly, parenting became considerably more complicated, and I was confronted with all sorts of dilemmas. Who would buy the vehicle? Who would pay for the insurance? What kind of auto? Cara and I decided that she'd buy the car and that her stepmother and I would pay for the insurance. Those determinations were relatively painless on my psyche. After all, they were just decisions. They weren't gas guzzling, oil dripping, broken down heaps crowding up the driveway.

The real pressure set in when I realized that, as the Dad, I was expected to chaperone this coming of age ritual in order to keep my daughter from "getting taken" by some wily, chops-licking, back-lot, used car salesman. I postponed the purchase of the auto as long as I could, with all sorts of lame excuses, contoured to calibrate miscellaneous weather conditions, like "Oh it's raining this weekend, it's bad luck to buy a car in the rain" or "Cara, it's such a beautiful day. Let's play tennis instead!" or "Wouldn't you rather I took you shopping for some new Guess jeans?" Obviously, I was trying to push back the inevitable as long as possible. But then, I had to decide if the hell of living with a sixteen year old who had her driver's license and no car was worse than the nightmare of having a clunker corroding in front of my house. I finally opted for the latter, as all dads do eventually . . . right?

Car Sick

This week we'll look
Long and far,
In every cranny and nook,
For you a car.

Whether it be a Chevy.
VW, Ford or Buick,
This week, I promise,
We'll go out and do it.

love (bug), dad

"Sometimes a poem is no place for an idea."

—*Edgar Watson Howe*

My father, whom I called "Pop," worked for Philip Morris Tobacco Company for forty three years as a shipping clerk. Every Friday, he'd come home from work with a special company "benefit," a free carton of cigarettes. He and my mom were both heavy smokers back then.

When eighteen, I won a four year Philip Morris academic scholarship to Wake Forest University in Winston-Salem, North Carolina. Ironically, Wake was heavily endowed by R.J. Reynolds Tobacco Company. Every month or so from my sophomore year on, Pop used to send me a "care package" consisting of a few packs of my favorite brand of Philip Morris cigarettes, Parliament. If I was going to smoke while away at a Tobacco Road school in the Tar Heel state, he didn't want me to turn traitor and start smoking Winstons.

I smoked, lightly, for about ten years. Still, any amount of smoking was too much for Margie. I can't remember if it was while we were dating, or after we'd just gotten married, but one day she announced that she was not going to kiss me any more, as long as I smoked. She said my breath, hair, and clothes reeked of cigarettes, and she wasn't going to subject herself any longer to that awful smell. So, I had a choice to make, kiss or whiff. I chose kiss.

Years later, every now and then, I'd get on my high horse and try to impart to the girls one of my firmly held, self-righteous beliefs about some current, controversial topic. Most of the time, they just took it all in and had little to say in response. But Cara remembered a bit of my tobacco stained history, and vividly recalled that familiar story of Margie's kiss ultimatum to me. So, on this occasion, when I used a napkin for an anti-smoking soapbox harangue, I hit a raw nerve with her. It's the only napkin on which she rebutted, in writing. She was calling me on the carpet, exposing the hypocrisy of her past puffing dad.

Former Smoker's Lament

When smoke fills the air,
Does the cigarette addict care
Where
That smoke goes?
Even if it's up
Someone else's nose?

love, dad

And Cara rejoined, "Did you?"

"Success consists in the climb."

—*Elbert Hubbard*

The success of our three *Hats in the Belfrys*, in Annapolis, Georgetown, and Harborplace, had attracted nationwide attention. Would-be entrepreneurs from Philadelphia, New Orleans, Houston, Minneapolis and Denver, having stumbled into one of our packed shops on a Saturday night while on vacation, and immediately recognizing the sizeable profit potential from such a mom and pop enterprise, yearned to open their own hat shops in their home cities. These wannabe hatters were eager to pay Margie and me for our expertise on how to start and operate a thriving retail business. In response to this broad demand, we decided to franchise the hat store concept and thus formed *Hats in the Belfry Franchise Corporation*. By 1987, we had fourteen franchises all over the country.

The press loved our shops. We were always doing crazy stuff, creating a corporate culture. One year in the early eighties, we noticed that our shops had made an incredible number of expensive hat sales to women who wanted to sport the look of Princess Di. Diana was a milliner's dream come true. So, we wrote Her Royal Highness, and invited her (and, yes, Charles too) to our home for dinner. The royal dinner invitation, and hopefully a visit from the future King and Queen of England, was to be our way of thanking Diana for wearing so many hats, and for looking so good in them. (She declined our offer).

Margie and I were frequently interviewed, and our American Dream story was included in countless newspaper and magazine articles. The fact that we were a husband-wife team who worked together almost every day caught the attention of an author writing a book about couples entitled, *In Love and In Business*. She asked and received permission to include our hat shop story in her book. To boot, that author invited us to accompany her on her national tour to promote the work. Consequently, Margie and I appeared on "Good Morning America" with Randy and Debbie Fields, of *Mrs. Field's Cookies*, and were questioned for eleven minutes by Joan Lunden, with Barbara Walters sitting a few feet to the left, slightly out of camera range.

A few weeks later, Dr. Ruth Westheimer had us on her show. It seemed to me that hat merchants surfacing on a sex show was a stretch, but I was mistaken. Dr. Ruth can find the lascivious angle to any subject. The way she saw it, Margie and I were on her show because we were "in love and in business," and if you were in love, you probably were in sex too. Ruth was intrigued by the idea of couples working together all day at the office, talking business at home after work until the wee hours of the night, and then sleeping with each other. When was there time for sex? Was there a code we used to let each other know that we were ready to switch gears, that we were tired of discussing hats and ready for making love? Never one to miss an opportunity for sexual titillation of her audience, Dr. Ruth looked at me with a twinkle in her eye and suggested, "Maybe Courtney, you have a special hat you wear up to the bedroom to *signal* Margie that you want to make love? Do you?" I couldn't believe my ears. A hat to intimate I wanted to be intimate? The live studio audience stirred and giggled with erotic anticipation. The sharks were circling. I was unnerved by this diminutive, elderly woman wanting to converse about my copulating conventions on network television. But I mustered all the courage I possessed and did the manly thing: I choked. My brain went dead. I couldn't think of anything to say in response. There was now total silence on the set as all eyes focused on me to come up with a zinger, but I was hopelessly flustered. I hadn't prepared for this line of questioning. I sank lower into my chair cushion and mumbled. Finally, realizing that I was not making good copy, the camera crew mercifully directed their focus onto some other hapless victim and left me alone.

Besides television appearances, another result of franchising was that I had to travel more, to all parts of the country to inspect prospective locations for future *Hats in the Belfry* franchises. When I was away, Margie would pinch hit for me with the kids. She always tried to do things for Adrienne and Cara the way I would have done them, but with a softer touch. At various times in the girls' lives, she picked them up from lacrosse practice after school, drove them to dentist appointments, fixed them delicious pasta with sauteed garlic and asparagus for dinner, read them Dr. Seuss bedtime stories (*Cat in the Hat*, what else?), helped with geometry homework, taught them how to tie their shoelaces, and supervised and fed a house full of kids whenever their friends visited. Margie was always there for the girls.

One time I was returning from a trip to Las Vegas, where I was meeting with shopping center developers who wanted our shop in their tenant mix. The meeting lasted longer than expected. I was anxious to get home, so I could see the girls before school the next day. The only flight available out of Vegas didn't arrive into Baltimore-Washington International airport until 3 A.M. I took it, but just couldn't get up three hours later to fix lunches. It didn't seem unnatural, therefore, the next morning, for Margie to get the kids up and off to school — and write them a napkin.

Just Plane Tired

Daddy's plane was so late
He doesn't even know the date.
He's sound asleep,
Not even a peep.

So I'm making lunch,
And I have a hunch,
It's not as good as his,
But it's all you get!

love, Margie

"You can learn many things from children. How much patience you have, for instance."

—*Franklin P. Jones*

I liked rock 'n roll music, and I liked it played thunderously. When a song moved me, it *physically* moved me, producing a harrowing degree of totally unattractive twisting and shouting to its blaring pulse. One day I was chauffeuring the girls back to their mom's, Adrienne in the passenger's front seat beside me, Cara in the left back seat, separated as far from each other as I could get them, so they wouldn't fight. Suddenly, barely audible over kid babble and traffic noise, the soul-shaking sounds of Tina Turner's "Better Be Good To Me" came cascading out of the radio. I cranked up the volume, kept time by bongo-drumming my hands on the steering wheel, bobbed my head, lurched my shoulders back and forth, flapped my arms like an Alaskan white swan drying his wings, perfectly imitated the "Elvis-the-Pelvis" hip wiggle a few times, and threw open my mouth. The harsh reality that I couldn't carry a tune in a wheelbarrow in no way inhibited me from vociferously serenading my captive audience. "Girls! This is a GREAT song! This is Tina Turner! Just listen to her legs, I mean…VOICE!" I'd exhort them as I rhythmically stomped my accelerator-free foot. Sometimes the girls would indulge me and bounce around a little, but often they just sat quietly, probably hoping that the next song would be "Taps" or some other funeral dirge so that their dad would quiet down and talk to them.

Therefore, when the girls reached that age whereby they were into "boom boxes" and loud music, I was naturally a little sheepish about protesting the amplification. To assuage my uneasiness, I convinced myself that it wasn't the volume in itself that bothered me about the girls' music, it was their choice of times to play that heavy metal discord, like while they were trying to study, for example. How, I wondered, could they simultaneously listen to that cacophony and concentrate on doing homework? And was there no awareness whatsoever in that

hormonal generation that other members of the household might be engaged in pursuits coun-
terproductive to The Psychedelic Furs' pulsations permeating the periphery? For many years, I
was confronted with the question: How many times, in how many ways, can a parent ask nicely for the kids to "Turn the damn stereo down!"

Household Harmony

The woods are full of trees,
The sky is full of clouds.
But do something for me please,
Don't play your music so louds!

love, dad

"You have two choices for lunch. Take it or leave it."
—*Paraphrase from H. Jackson Brown, P.S. I Love You*

By some, I was derogatorily labeled (libeled?) a "health nut," in part, perhaps, because I refused, most of the time, to make junk food available to my kids. Even in traditional candy traps like Christmas stockings and Easter baskets, I cut against the conventional corn. It's now a family legend, which Adrienne and Cara good-naturedly chide me about, how at those two special holidays, other kids received those sweet surprises like caramel bars, jelly beans, chocolate eggs, and sugar coated lollipops, whereas my girls were disappointed to discover juicy red apples, Florida oranges, and whole wheat granola bars in their stockings and baskets. I admit that I carried the health kick too far back then, but it does make for boring, humorless family stories today.

Being a vegetarian, I was especially concerned about the nutritional level of what I packed for the girls' lunches. I tried to make the food interesting, tasty, balanced, and meatless. But many a day, Cara opened her bag to curious cuisine. Often I would take a portion of the previous night's supper, plastic baggy the casserole concoction, and use that as the entree of that day's lunch.

Whereas I suspect most kids who brought their lunch from home discovered the traditional ham and cheese sandwiches, a piece of fruit, and maybe a cookie or two for dessert in their bags, Cara often unwrapped uneaten Broccoli Bake, Very Vegetable Chilly Chili, or remaining

Rosemary Roasted Potatoes as her main course, mozzarella cheese sticks or unshelled, unsalted Suffolk, Virginia peanuts for appetizers, and Dannon's fat free fruit yogurt or a maple syrup flavored, oatbran granola bar for dessert. Whenever I just couldn't figure out how to cater to her sweet tooth, I'd take the easy way out and give her money to purchase a cup of cafeteria ice cream.

I don't recall what I stuck into her lunch bag that inspired this poem. Maybe it was a brown banana, or half a cucumber sandwich. Whatever it was, it wasn't much.

You Are What You Eat

Don't mean to be a bore,
But today I do implore:
Buy yourself
Some dee-sert,

'Cause if you just
Eat this lunch,
You'll become in-ert.

love, dad

"Child raising is still a dark continent and no one really
knows anything."

—*Bill Cosby*

As the girls aged more deeply into their teens, sometimes I looked at what they thought about life and how they spent their spare time. Frequently, with frustration, I judged their basic belief systems to be rather shallow, extremely materialistic, self-absorbed, and disturbingly tuned in to immediate gratification, with little concern for either the past or the future.

I tried to get into their heads. I wanted to know what their ideas were about the world around them, about the controversial subjects being debated at that time: abortion, war and peace in Central America, the poor in this country. Alas, I was disappointed. Their world consisted primarily of typical teenage topics: cars, boys, friends, and money. They didn't see much use in thinking about the "grownup stuff" that I was interested in. Nor did they have much background knowledge with which to carry on any kind of meaningful conversation. Their education was primarily, as mine was, an exercise in memorization rather than critical thinking about tough issues.

For their age group, visual images evoked stronger emotions than the printed word. After all, they were the original MTV generation. Television became my ally during a few days of particularly disturbing current events, and I used it to prick Cara's conscience.

Tiananmen Tragedy

Nothing could be finer
than a morning in China
unless you get shot dead.

The students in Beijing (Bay-Jing)
say, "Let democracy ring!"

And then die
while they lie
in the hospital bed.

Love, dad

"Teaching a child not to step on a caterpillar is as valuable to the child as it is to the caterpillar."

—*Bradley Miller*

I continued to fret about what the younger generation was coming to, and decided that, wherever I could inject a bit of contemplation in my girls' lives, I would do it. The morning napkins seemed as good an opportunity as I would get. On one occasion when her history class was studying World War II, Cara seemed neither to grasp nor appreciate the horrors of war and oppression. I wanted her to imagine what life would have been like under those conditions.

Hell On Earth

How would you
Liked to have been a Jew
in 1942?

If German, your choices weren't so hot:
Concentration camp, gas chamber,
Or be shot.

No matter what you say,
A Jew was in a lot of danger,
Unless living in the U.S.A.

love, dad

"Just remember, we're all in this alone."

—*Lily Tomlin*

Adrienne had been spanked on her rear once when she was about three; Cara never. As a child, I had been struck with switches, belts, coat hangers and my parent's hands. I was never bruised, and these swattings were an acceptable form of child control when I was growing up. I always knew that my parents loved me. In fact, it was because they loved me and cared about my outcome that they used whatever means they could to make me "a good boy." As a parent and a student in the field of Human Development, however, I had learned that employing physical force against my child was not an acceptable method of behavior modification. Looking ahead to the day when Adrienne and Cara would be mothers, I wanted to instill in them my attitudes about corporal punishment.

No Excuse

Spank, hit, paddle and smack.
If your child acts contrary,
don't worry,
just give 'em a whack.

You may call it disciplin,
but that's just a ruse
for the much larger sin
of child abuse.

Love, dad

"Society is like the air, necessary to breathe, but insufficient to live on."
—*George Santayana*

Both the girls' sets of parents had worked hard for our lifestyles — and been lucky. Margie and I came from poor backgrounds. Our parents didn't give us much materially because they didn't have much to give. Now, we had achieved our parents' dreams for us: we were financially successful. We could afford to give the girls many of those material possessions our parents could not afford to give us. And, of course, Adrienne and Cara wanted it all.

The dilemma was whether to give them all we could afford to. Wasn't this what my parents had worked so hard for — to enable me to make things better for my children as well as for myself? But understanding the value of money — how hard it is to come by, how easily it can slip away — is one of life's valuable lessons. How were the girls to learn that lesson if they never experienced what it was like to earn money and then decide whether to save or spend it?

In the end, Margie and I split the difference. The girls bought their own cars and experienced the frustration of owning a heap. Their mother and I paid their initial insurance costs, but they would bear any premium increases due to speeding tickets or accidents. They received a moderate clothing allowance, but had to earn their own spending money.

Teaching fiscal responsibility to typical teenagers who were bent on fitting in with their peer group was a tribulation. Many of Cara's classmates *did* have a closet full of designer jeans and a new car of their own, thanks to mom and dad. One night Cara confronted me yet again with how liberal other parents were in lavishing big money items on their children. She made me feel cheap and defensive. I decided to challenge her.

Society's Child

Is the pressure to conform
a social ill?
Aren't we always compared
to the norm?

Aren't we pressured to meet
Others' expectations til
We can no longer take the heat?

Have no fears
About questioning your peers.

love, dad

"Let your capital be simplicity and contentment."
—*Henry David Thoreau*

It was a difficult concept to explain to Adrienne and Cara — why if we *had* the money, why we wouldn't use it to provide certain things to them, such as a new Mercedes (the car, the car, always the car!). I described how financially unstable a young retail business was, and that just because we had a few profitable years did not promise additional good years. In the case of a shortfall in sales, we would have to provide the operating funds out of past savings, and that meant we couldn't go wild with the money we currently possessed. We had to exercise monetary self restraint.

Then there was the concept of what money could or should buy. Margie and I didn't do a lot of things we could have done with our money. Many of the objects money could buy were things we didn't feel justified in obtaining. What we thought money could best be used to purchase was free time: if you spent most of your time on making money, where was the time to enjoy life? What good was life if there wasn't sufficient time to develop as a human being? We saw ample evidence that society was obsessed with attainment of material possessions at the expense of the important values. And I wanted to plant in the girls' minds the seeds that maybe what the culture bombarded them with really wasn't important to strive for after all.

Where You Goin' Girl?

What's your ambition,
Wealth and Fame?
Or is "the good life" just fiction,
The losing end of a game?

You work to a frazzle
Too tired to enjoy
Those diamonds that dazzle
and that new car toy.

Is this what you wished?
Is it worth what you bought?
Before you get squished,
Better give it some thought.

love, dad

"Your attitude, not your aptitude, will determine your altitude."
—*Zig Ziglar*

Admittedly, this was pretty heavy stuff for a care-free fifteen year old to appreciate, and I can't say with any surety whether my philosophizing napkins positively impacted on Cara at the time. Now that she's a twenty-five year old worker bee in the corporate world, laboring long hours and under considerable pressure, she seems to have a better grasp of what I was talking about then.

Being a believer in (although not a good practitioner of) "mind over matter," I did make, at that time, some half-hearted attempts to persuade Cara that she had power over her life, that perception mattered, that she could, to an appreciable degree, control her own reality by how she viewed situations.

One day, playing against the county's top high school lacrosse team, Cara had a miserable game. She missed three "free" shots on goal from just a few feet out, was reprimanded by the officials, and almost thrown out of the game for an illegal body check and, due to a defensive lapse, "allowed" her one-on-one opponent to score two goals. The Annapolis team lost 10 - 2. Afterward, Cara became despondent, and wondered out loud whether she had the skills to be a good lacrosse player. I knew she'd just had a bad game and, after a few days of licking her wounds, would bounce back. So, badly maligning my metaphors, I told her that she was probably feeling like a baseball batter who has just been thrown a "knock down" pitch while standing at home plate. What she needed to do, at this crucial juncture, was to get herself up out of the dirt, brush off her ego, get right back at the plate and wait for that home run pitch. If she believed she could do it, she could do it. Of course, still stinging from the hurts of the humiliating defeat, Cara wanted to feel a little sorry for herself. So, my words went to waste, *that* day. But that didn't deter me from trying again the next day to address one of Cara's few bouts of negativity about her lacrosse ability.

You're There, So Cross That Bridge

You are what you think you are.

So, what are your choices?
Saying, "I'm bad, I stink"
Or, "I'm good! I'm a star!"

Which of these voices
Will get you far?

Love, dad

"We find a delight in the beauty and happiness of children,
that makes the heart too big for the body."
—*Ralph Waldo Emerson*

Sometimes, the sheer emotion of being a father to such wonderful daughters just overwhelmed me, and I had to release these feelings or burst. It also helped that, as a tot, one of Cara's precious mispronunciations at breakfast occurred when she wanted "Syruple, Daddy! More syruple!"

Roses and Violets

The sky is blue,
And grapes are purple.
And I love you,
Like pancakes love maple syruple.

dad

"We are always too busy for our children; we never give them
the time or interest they deserve. We lavish gifts upon them;
but the most precious gift — our personal association, which
means so much to them — we give grudgingly."
                                                    —*Mark Twain*

I wanted the girls to know that they were on my mind even when they weren't visiting me. When they did stay over, I felt some degree of control over the direction of their development. Perhaps that was merely an illusion, but when they returned to their mother's, I felt a little isolated and out of touch with their lives. I remember, when I was a kid, going to spend every weekend and all summer with my grandparents. For many years, I loved it. They showered me with attention, had the money to buy me fun toys, and spoiled me. But around the age of thirteen, I resisted going to see them because I longed for the excitement of being at my own home. I felt I was missing something by being at "Nanny's and Grandaddy's" and, even though I wasn't quite sure what it was, I thought it must be good. I wanted my finger on the pulse of home life, and it seemed to be passing me by at my grandparent's house.

Likewise, when the girls were with me, I felt I had my finger, albeit loosely, on the pulse of *their* lives. Life was hectic, but I thrived on the chaos — the crazier the better. I felt secure. When they left, I sensed a disconnect from their vibrations. I enjoyed the peace and quiet of an empty nest, but yearned for the opportunity to influence the speed and drift of the girls' growth. I assumed that, if I were feeling detached from them, they, while with their mother, were probably feeling detached from me. I didn't want them to think that I'd forgotten them.

Out of Sight, Not Out of Mind

I love you so much
as much as the sky is blue.
And even when I'm out of touch,
I'm still thinking of you.

Love, dad

"If you bungle raising your children, I don't think whatever
else you do matters very much."

—*Jacqueline Kennedy Onassis*

Everything was not always sunny in father-daughterland. I remember the time when the graduating class at Cara's high school celebrated "Senior Hook Day" by having an unsanctioned party during school hours at a nearby park. Cara insisted that she be allowed to skip school and celebrate with the seniors, even though she was only a sophomore! Of course, I vetoed her petition. Then during her own senior year, Cara informed me that there was no longer *a* "Senior Hook Day" — now there were *ten* of them throughout the last academic term and, of course, she intended to miss class and party hearty at every one of them. Again, request denied. Finally there were instances when Cara tried my patience by feigning a head cold or sore throat and begging permission to stay home from school. I knew she simply had not done her homework the previous night and just didn't want to face her teacher's reproach. How the child graduated I'll never know. Sometimes I got fed up with the excuses and decided to adopt a harder line. After all, her future real life in the working, living-without-parental-support world, wasn't going to be so cushy. I felt like bellowing to her in my deepest baritone, "AS YOUR FATHER I FEEL COMPELLED TO TEACH YOU TOUGHNESS BECAUSE, YOU KNOW, IT CAN BE A HOSTILE WORLD OUT THERE AND YOU CLEARLY NEED TO LEARN SELF-DISCIPLINE AND DELAYED GRATIFICATION. AND I WANT YOU TO FEEL PROUD TO BE A GARTON BECAUSE WE GARTONS ARE STRONG!" But I resisted the soap box lecture and instead, wrote her an unsympathetic napkin one morning while she was upstairs moaning and muttering about "having the sniffles."

Sick and Tired

Even with a stuffed up nose
Off to schoolhouse you goes.
Because, you knows,
Life isn't a Rose
Garden,
Garton.

Love, dad

"The best way to keep children at home is to make the home atmosphere pleasant — and let the air out of their tires."
—*Dorothy Parker*

Dealing out discipline was my most flagrant fatherly flaw. It was difficult to be detached and cool under fire when Adrienne was slamming doors in a temper fit because I wouldn't let her stay out until midnight or Cara closed down and spoke curtly — and only when spoken to — because I had grounded her for some grievous infraction. Satan wasn't the role I had envisioned for myself in the family troupe. I wanted to be loved by my children. After all, I was their Father!

Doubt was my unflagging usher in deciding whether and what punishment suited their misconduct. Should I play God The Father and pronounce a punishment or allow the girls to experience the logical consequences of their mis-behavior? And what were the logical consequences of Adrienne's lying to me or Cara's deliberately disobeying curfews? Many times I charged headlong, headstrong, devoid of thought and reason, into an emotionally explosive situation. And the logical consequence of that behavior usually was unpleasantness.

During her sixteenth year, Cara's curfew was midnight on weekend nights. I would wait up for her, not being able to sleep until I knew she was safe in the house. At ten minutes past midnight, I'd start to worry if I hadn't heard from her. By twelve-thirty, I was fuming, and almost ready to call the police. Once she came traipsing in, laddy-da, forty minutes past curfew on a Saturday night. I was livid and laid into her about her inconsiderateness, intentional disobedience, and her low marks in algebra, just to make sure I hadn't skipped anything. Then I announced that she would be grounded a week for being late and not phoning me.

It so happened that there was a big dance coming up the following weekend. Because she really wanted to attend that special function, Cara complained all week about the grounding punishment being disproportional to her delinquency. After a few days of listening to her croplogic carping and unbroken begging to be taken off restriction so she could attend her showy shindig, I just decided to dig in my heels, play power ball and refuse her pleadings. She sulked and whined, but I made light of it by crooning The Rolling Stones' "You Can't Always Get What You Want" as I danced a little jig across the floor.

Big mistake! Cara didn't speak to me for a week. What wonders a daughter's cold shoulder can do to ruin a father's resolve! It's a miracle really how this phenomenon works. Suddenly I'm the bad guy for belittling her misfortune, and now I'm looking around for ways to get back in her good graces. Oh how easily the table of contrition turns. But, shouldering the adult role model mantle, (and wanting to regain my "Good Daddy" status), I did penance for making light of her situation.

Bully For Me

Your feelings I didn't respect —
I acted like a bully.
Sometimes even parents can't hold in check
Their errors in judgment fully.

So even though I treated you bad,
I am sorry and I do love you,
'Cause I am still,

Your Dad.

P.S. But, and not by chance,
    you still can't go to the dance.

"Cleaning your house while your kids are still growing,
Is like shoveling the walk before it stops snowing."
—*Phyllis Diller*

On another occasion, Cara and I had a typical dad-daughter confrontation about her "freedom." She properly informed me that she intended to pile five of her closest friends in the car and drive two hours to the beach for the weekend. Because she was only sixteen at the time, and had just received her driver's license the day before, I said "no way." Cara got mad and chastised me. By refusing her request for instant motorcar manumission, I, the Ogre Papa, was being "too strict," I never let her "do anything," and I was hopelessly out of touch with reality because "everybody else gets to go." Amidst that battering barrage of badmouthing, I clutched my convictions closely to chest and held on.

Hard To Make A Stand

There was once a mean old dad,
Who wouldn't let his daughter be free.

The daughter got mad,
The father got sad.

That's the tale so far, you see
For that mean old dad
Is me.

Love me,
Love me not,
dad

"Children aren't happy with nothing to ignore,
And that's what parents were created for."

—*Ogden Nash*

One of the most severe tests of my parenting life was when I had to reproach Cara. As a typical sensitive teenager, she wanted guidance, but bristled at judgmental accusations, even when she was dead wrong. If there were a particular behavior of hers I had a problem with, I'd want to talk to her about it. The usual format was that I would go upstairs to her bedroom, sit in the banana yellow, vinyl PacMan chair, and announce, "Cara, you and I need to talk." Most of the time, that pronouncement, by itself, was enough to clam her up completely. She knew what was to follow. I'd go on and on about my not appreciating the disrespectful way she had spoken to me when she and I had recently wrangled verbally about her chatting on the phone too late on a school night, or I'd enlighten her on the virtues of supporting her sister instead of exploiting every opportunity to snitch on her ("Dad, today in school, Adrienne stuck two gummy worms up her nose!"). Cara wouldn't want to talk about "this stuff" because she thought there was nothing to talk about. After all, these issues weren't bothering *her*, they were bothering me.

On rare occasions she might instruct (lecture) me on the proper way of broaching a contentious issue between us, a way which would elicit open, frank revelations from her, rather than defensive shut mouthings. "Dad, she'd counsel, I hate it when you preach. If you think all this talk does any good, I'm here to tell you that it doesn't. It does just the opposite - it turns me off and I tune you out!" Alas, I learned slowly, for more often than not, after we sparred, Cara would retort with the predictably teenage, tight-lipped, mono-syllabic "Yeah" after I had concluded my sermon with the quintessential, predictably parental "Now, do you understand me?" So, occasionally, I tried to improve on Cara's and my "failure to communicate" with a poem.

Sorta Sorting Things Out

You want one thing,
we want another.
How can we let you have your fling,
do your own thing,
and still be a good father and mother?

We have to say what we think is right.
Does it always have to end in a fight?

We're just trying to help you grow.
When you become a parent, you'll know
that we do it out of love —
not because we think we're above
        you.

Love, dad

"Children are natural mimics — they act like their parents in spite of every attempt to teach them good manners."

—*Ogden Nash*

Another homily invariably would transpire each time after my mother, "Nanny," came to visit from Richmond, Virginia. Adrienne and Cara were her first grandchildren, and they were her darlings. She championed their cause almost no-matter-what. So it hurt me to see Cara treat my mom discourteously by sulking at the dinner table, piddling at her food, and then bolting at the first opportunity, instead of being sociable and showing some interest in lingering and conversing with her grandmother. I had "spoken" to Cara about this several times, to little avail, so I ventured an admonition via a napkin.

Manners Matter

You don't engage in talk
After dinner. You take a walk,
Leaving guests at the table.

You <u>are</u> able
To do what's right,
But for now,
Your behavior's anything but polite.

It really is rude
To project such a mood,
To not sit awhile and chat.
People don't like that.

love, dad

"Children in a family are like flowers in a bouquet: there's always one determined to face in an opposite direction from the way the arranger desires."

—*Marcelene Cox*

When Cara was seventeen, she was a senior in high school and looking forward to going away to college. The problem was that she also thought it beneath her to study. It just wasn't hip to put forth effort in school. The result of her slacking off was a first marking period report card of B-C-C-C-D-D, well below the minimum three-point grade point average required by the University of Delaware. She really wanted to attend Delaware because her sister was there.

If Cara wasn't accepted into Delaware, the alternative was the local community college, Anne Arundel Community College or, as it's known around here, AACC. It's a fine school (Adrienne went there a semester before transferring to Delaware herself), but Cara had a very snobbish attitude. She thought that this community college was for dummies, and that she was quite above that level, thank you. So, when she came home with that lousy report card, I wanted to shock her into realizing that the chances of her attending a prominent, four-year university were shrinking fast, and that she'd better start hitting the books. This napkin really got her goat (and her attention too).

Cara's Song (and dance)

"Hey folks—Look at Me . . .
I've got a one-point-eight-three . . .

I'm cool and oh-so-free
Except . . .

I'm going to A-A-C-C,
Instead of U. of D."

love, dad

"Where's the man could ease the heart
 Like a satin gown?"

—*Dorothy Parker*

Around prom time, life with a teenage daughter really got peculiar. The week prior to her Senior Dance, Cara nervously fluttered about the house like a restive robin flittering around her baby-laden nest. The telephone rang more often than the Liberty Bell on the Fourth of July. Even Call-Waiting overloaded. Plans had to be drawn and quartered and redrawn, and a miasmic expectancy enwrapped everyone in earshot as the female adolescent spirit swayed fitfully. And all this before the dress had even been assessed.

That year, Cara decided that she'd shop by mail — that is, have the ballroom robe shipped in, try it on for size, ship it back if it fell short of expectations, and then mail-order another. As it turned out, I paid more in transportation charges than the frilly frock actually cost. If I had invested in overland carrier stock that year, I'd be a wealthy man today. So I thought Cara should hear what was on my mind.

♪ OH U.P.S.
(To be sung to the tune of "Oh Christmas Tree")

Oh U.P.S., Oh U.P.S.
Will you bring us yet another dress?

Everyday your truck pulls up,
Just as we're about to sup.
Oh U.P.S., Oh U.P.S.
Will you bring us yet another dress?

One was blue, but way too tight.
None of them did fit just right.
Oh U.P.S., Oh U.P.S.
Will you bring us yet another dress?

I'm going broke just paying freight,
Could you please decrease your rate?
Oh U.P.S., Oh U.P.S.
Can't you get me outa this mess?

love, dad

"Happy is he that is happy in his children."

—*Thomas Fuller*

Absolute love for the kids was my ideal. I aspired to loving them when they behaved unlovingly, supporting them even if I didn't agree with what they were thinking or doing, and letting go of my natural tendency to be controlling. I knew that most theories of good parenting held that when one's children turn into hellions, keeping their self esteem intact is of primary importance. To offset my lapses in preserving the girls' fragile self-images, I used the napkins to try to repair some of their papa-perpetrated ego damage with a few injections of unadulterated daddylove. The following three poems were written at different times on separate napkins.

MoonShine

When the moon shines bright,
And the stars all glow
Against the empty, dark night,
Then you'll know
How much I love you.

Hugs and kisses,
dad

SunShine

When the sun starts to blaze
you,
And gusts of wind blow strong,
This may really amaze you,
But I'll always love you
Right or wrong.

love, dad

StarStruck

You're as fine as fine can be,
You're a shining star.
I think that, you see,
'Cause I love you just the way you
are.

love, dad

"That it will never come again
Is what makes life so sweet."

—*Emily Dickinson*

Sadly, the final day of Cara's secondary school life meant the end of the napkin writing era for me. Off to college she'd go, and though I'd correspond often, and even insert a few choice "poems" into my letters, I knew things would never be the same again.

At culmination of the child rearing epoch, most parents probably fumble with the same mingled emotions of grief, relief and disbelief that I did. The sense of loss can stagger the giddy anticipation of the freedom to come. Cheer from the great weight of parental responsibility being lifted from my shoulders was sometimes dwarfed by misgivings about what would be left now to keep my feet on the ground. Were all these years of child-rearing really (finally) coming to an end? Was it too good to be true? Did I really want it to be true? Of course I did! I had been a successful father of two fantastic children. My goals had been met: The girls were alive, healthy, educated (almost), not-pregnant, and I had a good relationship with both. Before me now was the new challenge of being a father to adult women. Congratulations all around! The girls had made it! And I was free!

Napkins No More

It's your last day of high schoolishness
Now you're smart — no more foolishness,
and this napkin's the last you'll receive —
you finally get a reprieve.
But the end of writing them
I'm already starting to grieve.

I loved the 12 years of communication
And now those school days you'll leave
But that
is no reason for me to be bereaved
In fact
I do believe
It's time for celebrations.
So, C-O-N-G-R-A-T-U-L-A-T-I-O-N-S!!

love, dad

"The Past is history
 The Future, a mystery
 The Present is a gift.
 That's why we call it the Present."
                              —*Famous West African Saying*

Where Are We Now?

When she was sixteen, Adrienne spent a year in Madrid, Spain, as a foreign exchange student. She failed all her classes that year, but did become fluent in Spanish.

When she was nineteen, Adrienne and I travelled to Costa Rica and bummed around that beautiful country for ten days. I was interested in politics and the culture, but didn't speak the language, so Adrienne translated for me. We have many warm memories of that trip, including the morning an oinking pig woke us up as we slept on one of Costa Rica's many pristine beaches.

Later, as a student at the University of Delaware, Adrienne returned to Costa Rica to study for a semester.

In 1992, she graduated from Delaware with a B.A. in Spanish. Three years later she married Hector Cruz. Hector is a sweet, thoughtful, caring son-in-law, but I love him anyway.

Adrienne's been busy. In 1997, she earned her Masters degree in Spanish Literature and Pedagogy from Delaware. She is now a "Navy wife," and soon to be a mother to a baby girl, my first grandchild, Annabelle Courtney.

Adrienne and Hector live in San Diego, California, where she teaches Spanish at a nearby college.

Cara lived with me during the summers while she attended college. I fondly remember that time as our Dad-Daughter roommate days. I still have the note I found one day tacked onto my computer room door which read, "Dad — bird in here. Cara." Bird? Yep, there was a live baby bird in a basket on the floor. Cara had rescued it after it had fallen out of its nest. And I recall one late night when I came home and found a trampoline in the middle of the living room. She had liberated the springboard from our local trash dumpster. I had to jump through a few hoops that night just to get to the couch. And we always disagreed on the air conditioning. I usually wanted it off, she wanted it on. When I *did* want it on, I wanted the thermostat set at seventy-eight degrees; Cara wanted seventy degrees. One day I found out why we were so far apart in our comfort zone temperatures: Cara had piles of dirty clothes three inches thick covering every air conditioning floor vent in her bedroom. The air in that den of iniquity was stifling. No wonder I froze downstairs while she roasted upstairs.

Despite the summertime oxygen deprivation to her brain, Cara graduated, with honors, from the University of Delaware in 1995. She earned a B.S. in Business Administration, with a minor in Management Information Systems.

Since graduation, she worked for Andersen Consulting, in Philadelphia, Pennsylvania, as a consultant in their Human Resources Division, and is currently working for Mercy Health System as a Senior Compensation Specialist.

Cara resides in Philadelphia with her wonderful, three year old black Labrador Retriever, Maverick. He is the love of her life. No . . . actually, I think maybe her boyfriend, Sam, is the love of her life. Hmmm . . . who knows? Some things never change.

Right after college, both girls bought chic, new, shiny-black Honda Accords, complete with anti-lock brakes, airbags, and cell phones. I drive a paint-scarred, 1982 Volvo sedan. Its odometer has been stuck on 108,562 miles for six years, and its glove compartment is held together with two and a half feet of duct tape.

Twenty-year-old Black Night Stars and the Moon, Uh-Huh, died of old age last year. Jesse died suddenly a few weeks ago. He was only eight. Muskrat gained ten pounds gorging himself on Meow-Mix, and now is a couch potato fat cat. He watches television a lot, especially NBA basketball playoff games. Muskrat lives with Margie.

Margie and I divorced in 1995. We are still cordial business partners. Four years ago, as a volunteer, she co-founded the Anne Arundel County Conflict Resolution Center. She and the girls remain very close.

Franchising the *Hats in the Belfry* concept nationwide did not work out as planned. There is one successful franchise, the Harborplace shop in Baltimore. There are four thriving company owned stores, in Annapolis, Georgetown, Old Town Alexandria, Virginia, and on South Street in Philadelphia.

Our buyer and merchandiser, Cindy, has been with the company eighteen years. Our overall operations manager, Sabrina, will soon mark nineteen years with *Hats in the Belfry*. Both Sabrina and Cindy started with us as part time salespersons in the Annapolis shop. Our comptroller and resident computer expert, Clay, has been part of the company for twelve years. He is married to my sister Debbie, who has worked part time as our accounts payable associate for eight years. We will all celebrate *Hats in the Belfry*'s twentieth anniversary in March, 1998.

In my spare time, I serve as a volunteer on the board of directors of Grandma's House, a child care center in two public housing communities in the Annapolis area. I also love to play tennis with all my buddies at Truxton Park in Annapolis.

"It doesn't matter who my father was. It matters who I
  remember he was."

—*Anne Sexton*

Cara

Cara's Version

Tootsie Rolls! What Tootsie Rolls? Who is he kidding? Let me take this opportunity to clarify that my dad did NOT reward us with tootsie rolls on that infamous Bay Bridge Walk when we were little. The way I remember it (and believe me, I have a knack for remembering those torturous events that he put us through), is that we got *granola bars*. Not the soft, chewy, chocolate-chip granola bars that most kids ate — these were the rock-hard, crumbly, no-salt, no-sugar, health-food granola bars from Hell. He would say, "One more mile and you can have a granola bar." We would say, "We have to walk a whole mile AND eat a horrible granola bar?"

My dad did not believe in Tupperwear. He had no problem putting spaghetti, applesauce, or any other inappropriate food in a plastic baggy. I'm not talking about the sturdy, tight, zip-lock baggies. No, he would use those cheap, generic, folding, LEAKY baggies. To this day, I think Dad would put a scoop of ice cream in a baggy if he still packed my lunch.

I remember going to visit my Nanny (Dad's mom) in Richmond. If the weather was nice, she'd insist that Adrienne and I go outside to play. We'd want to play indoors or watch television, but she'd say, "You know, your dad and his brother used to play outside all day when they were your ages. They could entertain themselves for hours by flicking a piece of folded paper back and forth across the patio table with their finger. Why can't you girls do something like that?" Now, try to understand, I grew up in a world of high-tech computerized games — not silly paper football. No matter how hard we tried, Adrienne and I could not entertain ourselves outside for more than fifteen minutes by "kicking" around that stupid piece of padded, triangular shaped, pretend-football, notebook paper.

I think I was the only six-year-old who knew how to spell the word "hyper." Anytime I did anything other than sit still, my dad would look at me and say, "Cara, you're getting H-Y-P-E-R." I didn't know what hyper meant, but I definitely could spell it.

Do you have any idea what it's like to have a HEARSE as your family car? Not only was it a hearse, but it had wall-to-wall carpeting, curtains on all the windows (yes, CURTAINS), a *Hats in the Belfry* logo on the outside, and it was PURPLE! First of all, wasn't my dad ("Mister-I-Just-Want-My-Kids-To-Survive") worried about the lack of car seats or seat belts? Secondly, weren't there any governmental agencies who should have found something wrong with driving kids around in a vehicle used to transport dead bodies? I could have died from embarrassment!

When I was about four years old, I walked into my dad's place and stomped my foot. Very clearly, I said, "Tell me the TRUTH — is there an Easter Bunny or Santa Claus?" He tried to avoid the question at first, but I persisted. Finally he told me that they did not exist, that everyone just pretended that they did. I was sad but, to this day, I appreciate that my dad was honest and that I could trust him to always tell me the truth. The tricky part then was to play along with my grandparents all those years so they wouldn't know that I knew the truth. I was quite the actress at age four!

Did I mention that my dad used to read dictionaries for fun? Whenever I didn't know what a word meant, he would make me look it up. I would usually tell him I wasn't that interested in the meaning but then proceeded to look it up anyway. Of course, the description of the word always contained a bunch of new words that I didn't know the meaning of either, so I got frustrated and gave up. Then I would look over at him reading and highlighting and pondering words, and I would feel a little more inspired. Isn't it funny how powerful parents' actions are?

Despite my gripes, I feel very lucky to have had such an amusing, exceptional, unique, and intelligent dad. Whether we were singing "The Grocery Store Song," playing kickball in the neighborhood, unloading hat boxes, or just being silly, I always knew he loved me. Sometimes I was embarrassed around him, sometimes I was proud of him, sometimes I got mad at him, but I was never disappointed by him.

My dad and I have a great relationship today and he taught me a lot of important lessons about life. One lesson that he still preaches is that I shouldn't let my work stress me out, because it's important to have fun while I'm young. Kind of goes hand-in-hand with one of his many favorite sayings, "If it feels good, do it."

Hey! What was that about his not wanting us to get pregnant?

Adrienne

Adrienne's Account

What I remember most about my life with Dad is probably the number of times Cara and I would gasp, "Daaaaaaaaaaad!!!" in astonishment when he threw us for one of his many loops. He always did things more than just a little out of whack. Sometimes when he did, our eyes just popped out of our heads while a huge admiring grin spread across our faces. This book is a perfect example of what I mean. Most parents, I imagine, would be more than a little reluctant to share, **with the world**, these crazy little so-called "poems," written in the wee hours of the morning by a father who was just "winging it." This is NOT great poetry waiting to be discovered. This is not a man seeking glory and recognition for his lyrical beauty. This is, quite simply, a collection of stories that my father used to express himself to his daughters. Of this, he is not ashamed. Nor are we.

Growing up with my dad was certainly an adventure. I honestly have to say that there was never a dull moment, whether it was because of his preference in clothes, music, cars, anything. He is definitely eccentric. As a kid, riding around in a hearse was a ball. Calling him "CG" on a field trip for which he was a chaperone, was cool. My dad was *not* going to be called "Mr. Garton!" I was proud to have him as a father despite, and maybe even a little because of, his loony acts.

Once, sporting a pair of bright red leather, high-top Reebok tennis shoes, he came to my high school to give a speech on being a successful business owner. Everybody thought he was wild. On my tenth birthday, Dad decided to give me a sock-hop party — outdoors. He cut up dozens of large hat boxes, laid the cardboard pieces flat on the ground under the trees in our backyard, set up the stereo system, and presto, we had a twelve-foot-square, slightly raised, corrugated cardboard dance floor. He and I went to the record store and bought about fifty hit 45's with songs like "Lay Down Sally" and "YMCA," music which we both picked out. Most kids' parents liked the oldies or classical music. But my dad was hip. He was up on all the current rock and roll, so much so that he fit in almost completely with the other kids my age (except that he had a big, bushy beard).

But I didn't just love being with my dad because my friends thought he was neat. I admired him because he *tried*. Everything he did as a parent, he did to improve our lives, to make us happier, to teach us about life. The simple act of making us breakfast and lunch each day that we were with him showed us that he wanted to be a part of our lives. He *wanted* to participate in the mundane, daily routine of mornings before school. To most parents, I imagine, that morning mealtime ritual is a drag — to him, it was precious.

So, why didn't I save my napkins? I don't know. I suppose it's because I was a typical kid who didn't see their future value. I loved reading them. I shared them with my friends and sister every day. But then, I used them for what they were intended, and they eventually got thrown away. But I don't have to have an old shoe box full of faded, crinkled napkins to remember their messages. I think that who my sister and I are today is proof enough that they worked in the way my dad intended.

About to be a parent for the first time, I find myself remembering the little things that Dad always did to make us feel special. Like getting down on all fours in the thick-carpeted den and gently playing "rough-house" games with us (that he made up, and named, of course) such as "Roll-y, Pole-y" and "Easy One, Tough One." Or helping us lug our overflowing duffel bags to and from the car when we were coming and going. We hated trekking all our stuff back and forth every week when we'd visit. Dad knew we hated it, and tried to make the task less onerous by pitching in and experiencing it with us.

And singing us those dumb songs! He'd just compose them out of thin air! However, there was one in particular I loved, and begged him to sing it to me each time I saw him (until I reached thirteen, that is). It goes like this:

 *The Wittle Blue Man*

I wuv you, I wuv you,
Said the wittle blue man,
I wuv you, I wuv you to deff,
Boom boom.

I especially liked the "Boom boom" part.

These "little things" he did were just a few of his exploits to make us feel loved, to make us feel important. And no matter how old we get, he still does them. I try to remember this as I am about to embark on this adventure called parenthood, because if my husband and I can be even half the parent my dad was, and still is, well . . . that's all we could ever want.

"In the final analysis it is not what you do for your children but what you have taught them to do for themselves that will make them successful human beings."

—*Ann Landers*

About the Author

Courtney Garton earned degrees from Wake Forest University and the University of Maryland. He was a public school teacher and now owns and operates *Hats in the Belfry,* a small chain of retail hat shops. Courtney lives on the Chesapeake Bay in Annapolis, Maryland, and will soon be a first time grandfather. *Napkins* is his first book.